TEA
TEC
of
JESUS

HERMAN HARRELL HORNE

Foreword by Milford F. Henkel

KREGEL PUBLICATIONS
GRAND RAPIDS, MICHIGAN 49501

Library of Congress Catalog Card Number 64-16634

ISBN 0-8254-2804-1

First Edition 1920
Reprinted 1964
Reprinted 1968
Reprinted 1971
Reprinted 1973
Reprinted 1974
Reprinted 1975

TEACHING TECHNIQUES OF JESUS by
Herman Harrell Horne was published prior to 1971
under the title *JESUS: The Master Teacher.*

Printed in the United States of America

CONTENTS

CONTENTS

FOREWORD

Dr. Herman H. Horne was one of America's outstanding educational thinkers. He was a scholar, a philosopher, a gentleman, and a Christian. He was best known, perhaps, for his vigorous opposition to John Dewey and progressive education. Dewey was one of the leading proponents of Instrumentalism (progressive education), while Horne was a leading representative of the Idealistic philosophy of education. However, it is a mistake to consider Dr. Horne merely as an opponent of John Dewey. He is a great Christian educator in his own right and has written extensively in this area. Unlike many of the religious educators of his day, he resisted the tendency to substitute "the psychological wisdom of man for the operation of the Holy Spirit in moving upon the hearts of men" *(Philosophy of Christian Education,* p. 17).

It must be remembered, though, that Herman Horne was a philosopher and a layman, not a theologian. Horne does not profess to be writing a theological work; in fact, he states,

> Let me request critical reviewers not to judge the book by a viewpoint not its own, and condemn it because it does not say what they want said. Our viewpoint is not the content of the teachings of Jesus . . . but the form in which this content is cast . . . . It would be unfair to infer that the author does not hold certain Christological views because he is silent concerning them . . . (p. xi).

Some will have difficulty reconciling his concepts of absolute Idealism with evangelical Christianity. Nevertheless, he was a serious educator, a thoughtful Christian, and deserves careful consideration.

He is the author of more than twenty books and has contributed to *Monroe's Encyclopedia of Education, Nelson's Encyclopedia of Sunday Schools,* and the *Forty-first Yearbook of the National Society for Study of Education.*

One of his great masterpieces is the book, *Jesus the Master Teacher.** Herman Horne's influence upon evangelical Christendom is much greater than is often realized. Many have used the Evangelical Teacher Training Association book, *Teaching Techniques,* without realizing the great extent to which Horne influenced this work. The chapters in this book on the art of questioning and the use of the illustration are largely based on material taken from Horne's book, *Jesus the Master Teacher.* Having Horne's book in print again will make this material available in more complete form for the student.

Dr. Harold Mason, professor emeritus of Asbury Seminary, states, "He was the biggest available man to meet John Dewey head on." It was Dr. Mason who first urged me to read *Jesus the Master Teacher* about twenty years ago when I studied Christian Education under him at Winona Lake School of Theology. I remember being impressed at that time with the wisdom and sound ideas that this book contained. I must admit, though, that I wondered how many of these educational principles were found in the teachings of Jesus, and how many were simply the current educational teachings of the day. Recently, in reading this volume again, I was further impressed by the author's sound educational principles, but also with a sense that much of this book truly reflects the educational principles of our Lord and Master.

Dr. Horne approaches the Word of God reverently to discover what the New Testament has to say about the teaching methods of Jesus. He is not alone in his search to discover the teaching methods of Jesus. Many such books have been written since Horne's book appeared, and courses were added to the seminary curriculum on the

---

*Now published under the title, *Teaching Techniques of Jesus*

teaching methods of Jesus. In recent times these courses are no longer found in many seminary catalogs. Actually, many of these books and courses lost their popularity because they set forth man's wisdom rather than setting forth the teaching methods of Jesus as recorded in the Bible. Perhaps others have failed to do what Horne has done so successfully because they did not heed his injunction, "Let no one try it who is not both a Biblical scholar and an educator."

Others, in the search for the teaching methods of Jesus, have emphasized education, psychology, or philosophy. One book, recently reissued, is the *Psychology of the Christian Personality* by Ernest M. Ligon. This significant book reflects to a large measure the attitude of many toward the teaching concepts of Jesus. Ligon states, "It is the aim of this book to interpret the teachings of Jesus in terms of modern psychology" (p. vii). Ligon's work, while attempting to expound the Sermon on the Mount, interprets it in terms of psychology and pragmatic philosophy. While it is provocative, it is not a Biblical exposition of the teaching methods of Jesus. Horne's work is based on the Gospels, and he analyzes them carefully and thoroughly to determine how Jesus taught.

Horne stresses active learning and deals with reliable principles of education. The Sunday school teacher and the prospective teacher will not be the same after reading this volume. There is much that can be learned from Jesus' techniques of teaching — and this book is a masterful summary. The sobering fact is that this treatise has been available since 1920, but the principles enumerated here have scarcely been used within many evangelical churches. This new edition should be a blessing for each person who reads it.

Malone College   MILFORD F. HENKEL

PREFACE

Glover writes in his book, "The Jesus of History" (p. 84): "I have been treating him almost as if he were an authority on pedagogy. Fortunately, he never discussed pedagogy, never used the terms I have been using. But he dealt with men, he taught and he influenced them, and it is worth our study to understand how he did it—to master his methods."

In 1906 a volume of bibliography on "Jesus Christ Our Lord" by S. G. Ayers contained five thousand titles. The name of Jesus is more written about than any other in history. Where so much has been written, it is astonishing how little attention has been paid to the pedagogy of Jesus. A few books, like that of Hinsdale, 1895; a few articles, like that by Ellis, 1902; and a few occasional pages in larger works, as in Wendt, these are all. The bibliography at the end of our own accompanying study is conspicuously and suggestively brief. The pedagogy of Jesus is a discovered and staked-out but unworked mine. Let no one try it who is not both a biblical scholar and an educator. The following pages have only scratched the surface and uncovered a few leads.

One may well wonder why it is that, though books have been written about education since the Republic of Plato and about Jesus since the gospel of Mark, it is only the present generation that has seen books written about Jesus as an educator. Perhaps it is because those who knew about Jesus did not know about education, while those who knew about education did not know about Jesus. There may also have been the feeling that reverence for Jesus as divine was inconsistent with the study of his methods as a human teacher.

Probably an apology for studying the pedagogy of Jesus is not demanded by our day. Some may still feel that Jesus as a teacher should be only heard, not studied. But what if studying his methods unstopped our ears, opened our eyes, increased our skill—nay, even developed our reverence?

The aim of this series of studies is twofold: first, immediately, to see how Jesus taught, or is presented to us as having taught, and, second, ultimately, to influence our own methods of teaching morals and religion.

To accomplish these aims the apparatus of scholarship will be reduced to a minimum and simplicity of presentation raised to the maximum possible.

This is not so much a work to be read, or even a text to be studied, as a guide book to be followed in study classes. It is especially designed for discussional groups. I have declined to do all the student's work for him. The teaching attitude is maintained on almost every page.

The mode of presentation will, so far as possible, make the reader a sharer in the process of discovering the methods of Jesus as a teacher. This result will be accomplished by first raising questions, then giving the reader a chance to answer them for himself, and then presenting the material and reaching our own conclusion.

The literature of the subject, all too brief, will be utilized in reaching our results, which, however, must rest back mainly and finally upon the four gospels themselves as our source material.

Into the credibility of the gospels, especially the Fourth Gospel, as presenting the teaching methods of Jesus, without, however, intending so to do, we do not enter, as not essential to our twofold aim indicated above.

Let me request critical reviewers not to judge the book by a viewpoint not its own, and condemn it because it does not say what they want said. Our viewpoint is not the content of the teachings of Jesus, where all the controversies rage, but the form in which this content is cast. Manifestly, it would be unfair to infer that the author does not hold certain Christological views because he is silent concerning them, and then condemn the book because those views were not defended.

This material has previously been presented in the Summer School for Christian Workers of the Auburn (N. Y.) Theological Seminary, in the Southern Assembly at Monteagle, Tenn., in the Eastern Association Summer School at Silver Bay, N. Y., in the Drew Theological Seminary, and in the Newark Community Training School. It is now put into printed form "by request," and also because it is the author's sure conviction that our methods of moral and religious education will not be perfected until we have sat at the feet of Jesus—the Master Teacher.

The quotations from President G. Stanley Hall indicate that he has helped me to see Jesus as the Great Teacher, though I do not accept his two essential conclusions that the real Christ is psychological and that religion is racially subjective.

In a field of scholarship so old, and yet from the standpoint of modern pedagogy so new, may I request readers to favor me with both corrections and suggestions?

And you, who at any time have worked with me through portions of this material, please receive this text in your hands with the author's personal greeting and thanks!

H. H. H.

CHAPTER I

THE TEACHING SITUATION

We are going to study "how Jesus taught." This implies that he was acquainted with the teaching situation, even that he was a part of it, and faced its problems; that he was confronted by the same kind of difficulties in teaching as we, if not the identical ones. That he clearly sensed teaching as a problem appears in his (or Mark's?) parenthetic injunction: "Let the reader note this" (Mark 13: 14, Moffatt) and in the Parable of the Sower, which was not given a title by Jesus, and which might perhaps better be called the Parable of the Soils. It exemplifies four kinds of pupils.

Now what are the elements essentially involved in the teaching situation?

It is an easy question, and, if the reader would be an independent student, let him pause here and first make the analysis for himself, and then read on. It will help you to recall the famous definition of a college (who said it first?) as Mark Hopkins on one end of a log and Garfield on the other. But though the "Log College" is famous in Princeton history, the college on a log is no longer reputable in these days of rich endowments.

The teaching situation involves: (1) a teacher (Hopkins); (2) a pupil (Garfield), or pupils; (3) environment (the log), which may be amplified to include classroom, laboratory, library, apparatus, etc., even the social *milieu;*

1

(4) curriculum, or thing taught; (5) aim, or that which the teacher would accomplish by means of instruction in the life of the pupil, and (6) method, or the way of the process.

Can you think of any additional essential thing, like organization, management, discipline?

Or, can these six be further reduced?

Were the teaching situations in which Jesus found himself ever complex enough to contain these six elements? The scene of Jesus and Nicodemus, perhaps, under the olive trees at night on the mount near Jerusalem, is similar to Hopkins, Garfield, and the log. Jesus was the teacher, addressed by the pupil, Nicodemus, thus: "Rabbi, we know you have come from God to teach us." The environment is that night scene, protecting a distinguished but timid and fearful pupil. The subject of instruction is "the birth from above." The aim of the teacher was, probably, to effect a great change in the life of his pupil. (Was this aim accomplished? See John 7: 50 and 19: 39.) The method used was conversation, including question and answer and a remarkable concrete illustration of the working of the Spirit (John 3: 8), and the exhibition of surprise.

At this point pause a few minutes and analyze another one of the teaching situations in the life of Jesus, e. g., that with the Woman of Samaria (John 4: 1–42) or that of the Great Confession (Matt. 16: 13–28).

In fact, would it not help us to make a list as complete as possible of all the leading teaching situations in the life of Jesus?

Would it be proper to regard the miracles he wrought

as teaching situations? (For answer, see Mark 2: 10 and study Luke 5: 1–11.) Why?

If the miracle situation is not to be regarded as primarily a teaching situation, may it be so regarded in a secondary sense? Why? This question implies that the miracles may have taught the people lessons without being wrought mainly for that purpose. If not to teach, what was the main purpose of the miracle? This question may be passed over as irrelevant for the present, though important.

We get the unavoidable impression that Jesus was repeatedly involved in teaching situations and that in each of these some method or methods were used. Passing by for the most part the other five elements in the teaching situation, the following studies will concentrate mainly on the *methods* Jesus used as a teacher. There is no reason why a corresponding study should not be made of each of the other five elements. Why should not somebody undertake it?

CHAPTER II

AN OBJECT LESSON IN TEACHING

Later we shall take one principle of teaching and seek illustrations of it in the work of Jesus. Now we propose at the outset to take one section of his work, a unity in itself, and find in it some of the principles and methods of teaching he utilized. It will give us an aviator's view of the field.

Not that Jesus ever taught to give us an object lesson in teaching, though he did wash the disciples' feet to give them an object lesson in humility, but that we can use such masterly lessons as he gave his pupils as models for our own study.

What would be a good illustration to take? Select your own and find in it all the principles of teaching you can.

Let us choose John 4: 1–43.

Topic: How Jesus Taught the Woman of Samaria.

1. Here we have a *complete* teaching situation, with master, pupil, environment, subject matter, aim, and method. Jesus is the master, the woman of Samaria is the pupil, Jacob's well is a part of the environment, the water of life is a part of the subject matter, the transforming of a life is the aim, and what are the methods?

2. The Master utilized an *occasion* as it arose, though he was weary with his journey, and it was the noon-hour, and she was a Samaritan and a woman, and sinful.

4

There were several reasons why he might have let this occasion slip, but not so. "There cometh a woman."

3. He established a *point of contact*. She had evidently come to draw water. "Jesus saith unto her, Give me to drink." He was thirsty; it was a natural request.

4. He had her *attention* and *interest* from the start. He had done an unexpected and unusual thing. He utilized "surprise power." Though a Jew, he had spoken to a Samaritan. This attention and interest are sustained throughout, even increasing in concentration and intensity as slumbering impulses are awakened.

5. He used the *conversational* method. Seven times he addressed her and six times she replied, the arrival of the disciples interrupting the conversation.

6. He was here dealing with an *individual*, though thereby the way was opened to deal with the *crowds* of the city for two days.

7. He exemplified the principle of personal *association*, for a brief time, by intimate converse with a woman who was a sinner, thereby causing his disciples to marvel.

8. He asked her no question, but he *answered* three of her explicit questions, as well as the deepest longing of her nature. He built upon her answers and made the most of them: "In that saidst thou truly."

9. There are *problems* at the basis of this teaching. First, there is the personal problem of the woman's life. Who was more conscious of this at the first, the woman or Jesus? It was his object to awaken her conscience. Then there is the theological problem, felt and stated by the woman: Where shall God be worshiped? She seems to have introduced this problem as a distraction from the

personal issue, but the answer of Jesus, "in spirit and in truth," reopened the personal problem.

Are there still other problems here? What?

10. His reply concerning the nature of worship and God is perhaps long enough to be regarded as the nucleus of a *private discourse*, with a single auditor. How did John learn about this conversation, do you suppose?

11. There is the use of *apperception* in passing from water to "living water," yet it is clear that even so the woman did not understand. (See v. 15.) There is apperception also in Jesus declaring himself to be the Messiah to one who said she knew that Messiah cometh (vv. 25, 26), and this time she evidently understood.

12. His use of the *concrete* appears in "to drink," "this water," "thy husband," "five husbands," "this mountain," "Jerusalem," "I am he." The concrete water of Jacob's well was used to illustrate the abstract water of life.

13. His use of *contrast* appears in the difference between "this water," after taking which one thirsts again, and his living water, after drinking of which one shall never thirst (vv. 13, 14). Also between the ignorant worship of the Samaritans and the intelligent worship of the Jews (v. 22).

14. His use of *motivation* appears in the awakening first of interest and then of conscience and finally of service. The conversation concerning water awakened interest, that concerning the husband awakened conscience, that concerning true worship awakened service. She carried back in haste to the city not the waterpot she had brought forth, but the living water.

15. Jesus secured *expression* from this voluble, motor-minded woman, first in words and then in deeds. He pierced the crust of her encased conscience by a command to act: "Go, call thy husband, and come hither." A motor command which could not be executed is the profound way in which the Master threw this precipitate will back upon itself in shame and confusion. Unintelligently she said: "Sir, give me this water"; intelligently she said: "Sir, I perceive that thou art a prophet." From superficial questions of curiosity her self-expression passes to serious concern in personal and religious matters, and finally to the ministry of Sychar.

16. Some striking *characteristics* of Jesus as a teacher appear in this incident, such as his disregard of current conventionality in talking with a Samaritan and a woman and a sinner; the absence of false modesty; intimate knowledge of his pupil (how did Jesus know the woman had had five husbands?); profoundest knowledge of his subject—the nature of God as spiritual; the demonstrated ability to teach; prophecy—"the hour cometh"; and self-assertion: "I that speak unto thee am he."

What impressions do you get from this evidence of teaching method in a single incident?

Do you feel that any one of these sixteen points is not really to be found in the case?

Would you add still other evidence of teaching method?

Take another one of the several longer conversations of Jesus, and see what principles of teaching you can find there also.

Is it better to study one teaching incident in the light of the principles or to study one principle at a time in the light of many illustrative incidents? In the former case there is repetition of principles as we pass from incident to incident; in the latter case there is repetition of references to the same incidents as we pass from principle to principle. Which method does this book mainly follow?

Take the conversation with Nicodemus and work out results similar to the ones above.

CHAPTER III

HOW DID JESUS SECURE ATTENTION?

When one mind approaches another for any reason, the first thing to do is to catch attention. Ordinarily in human intercourse this is done by a word, gesture, or touch. The need of winning attention and of keeping it is felt, not only by the teacher before his class, but by the preacher before his congregation, the lecturer before his audience, the lawyer before his jury, the salesman before his purchaser, and the writer and the advertiser, though only the printed page is before their readers. Anybody who influences anybody else must first have their attention.

Did Jesus have the attention of his auditors, even of those who did not hear him, but only heard of him? Who since his day or before has so had the attention of mankind? Stop a few minutes to think your answers to these questions.

Now why was this? How did Jesus so capture the attention of his generation, and, we may add, of all generations? For he is a teacher of the world.

Before answering this question directly, we must approach it by asking another: What kind of attention did people give Jesus?

Attention
{
Voluntary.
  With effort.
Involuntary.
  Without the sense of effort.
  With interest.
}

This diagram shows us the two main kinds of attention. One is voluntary, given with a sense of effort, because the object attended to is uninteresting in itself, though recognized as important. Or, voluntary attention may be given through fear of the consequences of inattention. Thus a boy may give voluntary attention to the multiplication table.

Involuntary attention is that given without the sense of effort to an object interesting in itself. It may lead one to put forth much endeavor, but without the hard sense of effort. So one may read an interesting story till late at night.

There are refinements upon these two kinds of attention which the psychologists make, into which, however, we do not need to go. For example, some loud, sudden stimulus, as the banging of a door, may make us attend involuntarily. And attention that began by being voluntary may, through the awakening of interest in the subject, pass into the involuntary, as Latin composition may become more interesting as we proceed to master it by effort. It is also to be noted that involuntary attention may lead us to expend considerable energy, but such expenditure is not accompanied by the distasteful sense of effort. Thus an interesting walk may take us farther and with less fatigue than an unwelcome errand.

Psychologists have a way of giving familiar terms somewhat unfamiliar meanings. We may not like this, but it is an aid to definiteness in psychological science. For example, we may ordinarily think of a thing done voluntarily as done willingly and done involuntarily as done unwillingly. Thus, if a boy goes voluntarily to school, he does not have to be sent. But these meanings do not fit voluntary or involuntary attention; rather the opposite. Voluntary attention, with effort, may be attention given unwillingly, while involuntary attention, with interest, is likely to be given willingly.

Now, in the light of these brief, bare statements about attention, what kind of attention did Jesus receive? What kind did his disciples (learners) give him? What kind did the Pharisees give him? Who that came to scoff remained to pray? With what kind of attention did they begin and end?

These questions you will probably find no trouble in answering yourself. Jesus received both kinds of attention. His willing disciples attended involuntarily. His unwilling auditors and critics, hearing him, not because they wanted to obey, but to entrap him in his talk, gave voluntary attention. Pilate's wife, but glimpsing him perhaps, gave involuntary attention. Pilate, with no interest in the proceedings instituted by the ecclesiastical Jews, but rather a distaste for the whole business, gave voluntary attention. Those sent to take him, returning without him, but with the reason that "never man so spake as this man," began with voluntary and ended with involuntary attention, as did those Jews who believed in him secretly, not openly, for fear of the ridicule of their fellows. The multitude gave him involuntary attention, "hearing him gladly." His fellow-townsmen, with "eyes fastened upon him" in the synagogue, began by giving him involuntary attention, though it passed into attention of the voluntary type as they drew back from the greatness of his claim. Some of these statements may not be just correct.

What kind of attention was that of Nicodemus? of the woman of Samaria? of the men of Sychar? of the Gadarenes? of Herod? of Mary, the sister of Lazarus?

Now, how did Jesus secure attention? It was no great problem to him. "He could not be hid." He secured attention because first, there were many things about him to interest people; second, he knew what to do to get attention.

What are some of the things he did to get attention?

He called for it. "Hear," "hearken," "behold," "give ear," he would say.

He announced his coming to any city by messengers in advance, sending forth the disciples into every city whither he himself was about to come.

He utilized posture—not that he ever posed. "When he was set [the position of the Oriental teacher], his disciples came unto him, and he opened his mouth, and taught them." He would sit in a boat on the lake and teach people on the shore.

He spoke in concrete, pictorial, imaginative language, which easily catches and holds the attention, as a moving picture does today. The phrase "fishers of men" may rivet the attention like a fixed idea.

He used the familiar to explain the unfamiliar. Thus, he said men do not put new wine into old bottles to explain why he and his disciples, contrary to the custom of John and his disciples, did not fast. Professor James says: "The new in the old is what excites interest." Did Jesus exemplify this canon? Can you illustrate your answer?

In teaching he did not belabor a point, but passed quickly from one phase to another of his general topic.

Thus, the different brief beatitudes. So, too, parables were spoken successively, one story after another, as The Lost Sheep, The Lost Coin, The Lost Son. Here is unity in variety. Professor James also says: "The subject must change to win attention."[1] Does Jesus exemplify this maxim? Can you give other illustrations?

Jesus also won attention because his teaching was so different from that of the scribes. "He taught them as one having authority and not as their scribes." Why will men listen more readily to one who speaks with authority (the prophet) than to one who speaks for the authorities (the priest)?

We may also say that Jesus received attention because he paid attention. He saw and was interested in what people were doing and saying, and in their needs, and in helpful sympathy he drew his soul out unto them. His works prepared the way for his words.

And people gave him attention because he was a peripatetic teacher. He taught as he journeyed from place to place. "We must go also into the next towns," he would say. Protagoras, the Greek Sophist, and Aristotle, the Greek philosopher, walked with their pupils within enclosures. Jesus walked with his pupils in the open, carrying his good news to all.

But mainly Jesus won attention because of that complex thing, covering a number of the preceding points and others besides, which we call personal magnetism. The sum of his qualities made him unique, matchless, winsome. People would say he had not learned letters

---

[1] See James, "Talks to Teachers," Chaps. X and XI.

in the rabbinical school in Jerusalem, that he came from Galilee, not Judea, that he was a Nazarene, that he was more than a match for the scribes, that he was followed by crowds, and that he was always doing and saying wonderful things.   In short, it was the personality of Jesus that attracted the attention of men.

Not that Jesus was, and did, and said, all these things consciously and intentionally to get the attention of men. Winning and keeping attention was probably no conscious problem to him at all.   He simply and naturally did those attention-winning things which poorer teachers must do with set purpose.   Thus we must consciously imitate him as our unconscious model.

Can you now think of still other ways in which Jesus won attention?

The point that it was mainly through personal magnetism that Jesus secured attention, just as any good painting of him today arrests our attention, leads us naturally to ask: What in Jesus interested people?

Suppose you had the privilege of preferring one request to Jesus face to face, what would it be?   Or, of asking him one question, what would it be?   What question would you like to ask Socrates?   Think the answers to these questions.   They will disclose to you the deeper sources of your own interest in Jesus.

The personality of Jesus was so striking that men, with their expectation of a Messiah to come, would say of him, "Can this be Messias?"   "When Messias cometh, will he do more wonderful things than this man?"   But others would say, "He is a Samaritan and hath a devil."   So the people of Palestine were interested to place Jesus correctly in their view of life. It was the habit of Jesus to let the people freely see in him the Messiah for whom they looked, rather than publicly to proclaim it, though he did the latter also, by implication, in the Nazareth synagogue. So his Messiahship interested the people.

Along with this went his claim to be able to forgive sins on earth. He even taught his disciples to bind and to loosen on earth. This is an arresting claim which would naturally concern the people in a practical way and their rulers in a theological way.

Then, too, the exalted content of his message interested the people. Accustomed to legalism as they were, here was a teaching of love that fulfilled all law, of mercy that was more than animal sacrifice, of a loving Father who saved and did not condemn the world.

Also they were attracted by the wonderful signs he wrought, which he did in loving and helpful sympathy, not at all to convince people of his Messiahship. In fact, the crowds would so follow him because of his wonderful works and to get the loaves and fishes and be filled, that it was his custom often to forbid the miraculously healed people to tell any man. This, however, only caused some to publish it yet the more. So the fame of him would spread as a wonder-worker, but he knew the people and would not trust himself to those who had no better basis for belief in him. So Herod in his palace had heard of him and had desired in kingly curiosity to see some magical work by him. This, together with Herod's evil treatment of John, so filled Jesus with indignation and contempt that "he answered him never a word." It was one of the times when even the silence of Jesus spoke with flaming tongue. But unquestionably the people were interested in Jesus as a wonder-worker, though he did not care for such regard.

A thing which always characterized Jesus, and which never failed to interest high and low alike, was his social freedom. He mingled with publicans and sinners, ate with them, received them, was known as their "friend," and so scandalized the leaders. But he was equally at home in the house of Simon the Pharisee at Bethany, and while there permitted gracious social attention from a forgiven sinful woman. Besides, though keeping both letter and spirit of the law of Moses, he paid no attention to the traditions of the elders about ceremonial cleansings of pots and vessels, and eating with washed hands, and not husking grain on the Sabbath day, and the like. He was above the established good usage, both religious and social, of his day. This social freedom which he exemplified interested everybody.

What additional things about Jesus would naturally interest people? The fact that to some he extended a definite call to be with him? His moral earnestness? How would you explain the fact that the young fishermen accepted his invitation at once? How that the young ruler declined? What do you suppose would have happened if Jesus and Saul of Tarsus had met face to face in the flesh? What do you think would happen now if Jesus should visit in the flesh one of our towns or cities, as he visited Capernaum or Jerusalem? Would he have our attention? In what about him would modern Americans be interested? How much has human nature changed in nineteen centuries?

We have now seen in a measure how the problem of attention and interest was solved in the teaching of Jesus. Make a list of the points he exemplified which we may imitate more or less in our work as teachers. Do you find that it brings Jesus too near or makes him too real in flesh and blood to study him in this way? If so, be patient till you are through, and then see what happens.

What was the effect on the lives of Peter, Andrew, James, John, and the other disciples, of their interest in Jesus? Did following out this interest soften and weaken their lives? Is it only by doing hard, disagreeable tasks that our lives are disciplined? Is there a discipline of higher interest as well as of effort? Did Jesus assign weary tasks as such to discipline his pupils? Think out these answers, and recall present-day discussions about the "soft pedagogy" of interest and the "hard pedagogy" of effort and discipline.

What do you think of this conclusion: The interest of his learners in Jesus led them to make the supreme effort of their lives? As fishermen they would never have expended nervous and muscular energy to the same extent that they did as followers of Jesus. The pedagogy of Jesus was not the soft pedagogy of interest alone, nor the hard pedagogy of discipline and effort alone, but the combined pedagogy of *effort through interest*.

For a discussion of Attention, see one of several monographs on the subject, as those by Titchener or Pillsbury, or any standard psychology, as those by James, Ladd, or Angell, or any educational psychology, as those by Thorndike, Starch, or Horne.

CHAPTER IV

HIS POINTS OF CONTACT

It is essential in all effective teaching that points of contact be established between teacher and taught. By a "point of contact" in teaching we mean how minds come to meet, the common meeting places of mind with mind. Just as we "rub elbows" in the physical world, so minds have points of contact in the mental world. Usually these points of contact are matters of common or joint interest. The one who establishes the point of contact knows the other so well or so sympathetically that he catches him where he lives. To do this involves adaptability and tact on the part of the teacher. He must be thinking about his pupils or his auditors or the other fellow, as well as about what he himself has to say or do. It is very difficult for a self-conscious or an awkward person to make contacts. He is like a defective electric light bulb—there may be physical contacts, but no flashes of light. Can you recall some one who is happy in establishing points of contact? How does he do it?

That such mental meeting places are requisite at the opening of any exchange of ideas is obvious. Without them the auditor may or may not be a party to the transaction, what is said may go "over his head," or make no real appeal to him at all. But once two people feel they have common interests, there is a basis for further transactions. Without the sense of contact established, two minds may pass as ships in the night without speaking. One of the commonest ways of getting together mentally is by a story, incident, or bit of humor. One of the best ways is to play together. What other ways can you think of?

Now, did the Master Teacher also establish points of contact? Read the following passage carefully and note the answer.

Next day again John was standing with two of his disciples; he gazed at Jesus as he walked about, and said "Look, there is the lamb of God!" The two disciples heard what he said and went after Jesus. Now Jesus turned, and when he observed them coming after him, he asked them, "What do you want?" They replied, "Rabbi" (which may be translated, 'teacher'), "where are you staying?" He said to them, "Come and see." So they went and saw where he stayed, and stayed with him the rest of that day—it was then about four in the afternoon. One of the two men who heard what John said and went after Jesus was Andrew, the brother of Peter. In the morning he met his brother Simon and told him, "We have found the messiah" (which may be translated, 'Christ'). He took him to Jesus; Jesus gazed at him and said, "You are Simon, the son of John? Your name is to be Cephas" (meaning 'Peter' or 'rock').

Next day Jesus determined to leave for Galilee; there he met Philip and told him, "Follow me." Now Philip belonged to Bethsaida, the same town as Andrew and Peter; he met Nathanael and told him, "We have found him whom Moses wrote about in the Law, and also the prophets—it is Jesus, the son of Joseph, who comes from Nazaret." "Nazaret!" said Nathanael, "can anything good come out of Nazaret?" "Come and see," said Philip. Jesus saw Nathanael approaching and said of him, "Here is a genuine Israelite! There is no guile in him." Nathanael said to him, "How do you know me?" Jesus answered, "When you were under that fig tree, before ever Philip called you, I saw you." "Rabbi," said Nathanael, "you are the Son of God, you are the king of Israel!" Jesus answered, "You believe because I told you I had seen you under that fig tree? You shall see more than that." He said to him, "Truly, truly I tell you all, you shall see heaven open wide and God's angels ascending and descending upon the Son of man."—John 1: 35–51 (Moffatt's translation).

As a matter of fact, did Jesus establish contact with the two disciples of the Baptist (Andrew and John), and Peter, and Philip, and Nathanael?

How then did he do it? Read the passage again carefully and make a list of your answers.

Now compare your list with the one following:

1. Jesus walked where his presence could be noted by the Baptist.

2. He used his eyes. He "observed" Andrew and John coming after him, he "gazed" at Simon, he "saw" Nathanael approaching, and had previously "seen" him under that fig tree in meditation, like Buddha under the Bo tree.

3. He opened up conversation, with the two, with Simon, with Philip, with Nathanael.

4. He asked questions. "What do you want?" "You are Simon, the son of John?" "You believe because I told you I had seen you under that fig tree?"

5. He invited companionship. "Come and see." They stayed with him the rest of that day. "Follow me."

6. He utilized the power of the name. We all like to

be recognized, and called by name. Further, in handling
the name, he took a personal liberty in an acceptable way
with a sense of humor. "You are Simon, the son of John?
Your name is to be Cephas."

7. He understood character, and showed that he did.
"Here is a genuine Israelite! There is no guile in him."
That astonished the doubting Nathanael. The open
compliment was not lost on him. His pride was perhaps
tickled as he recognized himself under the fine tribute.
He began to capitulate. Somewhat bluntly, without address, he asked: "How do you know me?" The answer,
showing that Jesus had noted him under that fig tree in
pious meditation, appreciating Nathanael at his strongest
points, led to immediate and unconditional surrender:
"Rabbi, you are the Son of God, you are the king of
Israel."

It is small wonder that a teacher who could establish
such contacts had loyal followers. Even so, it is possible
Peter, Andrew, and John were called again, or even a
third time. (See Mark 1: 16-20, and Luke 5: 1-11.)
Study these passages. Compare the points of contact.
How many different calls to discipleship did Peter, say,
receive?

How did Jesus establish a point of contact with the
woman of Samaria? See John 4: 1-42, especially verse 8.
It was a natural request for a favor. It was so simple.
Yet it surmounted two high walls of separation, that
he was Jew and that she was scarlet.

Nicodemus seems to have felt under the necessity of
establishing a point of contact with Jesus. How does
he do it? See John 3: 2. Did Jesus require such a mode

of approach? Do you think Jesus interrupted his speech? Evidently at some previous time the mind of Nicodemus had opened to Jesus. How do you imagine it may have come about?

How did the Pharisees and Herodians seek a point of contact with Jesus? (Matt. 22: 16.)

The rejection of Jesus in his home town, "where he had been brought up," must have been a sorrowful disappointment to him. Was his point of contact successfully established? What was it? Read very carefully Luke 4: 16–30. What caused them to reject him after speaking well of him and marveling at the gracious words that came from his lips? The trouble here seems not to have been with the point of contact, which was the prophecy of Isaiah and its fulfilment.

How did Jesus establish contact with the thirty-eight-year invalid at the pool of Bethesda? See John 5. "Wouldest thou be made whole?" is the question approach on the matter of keenest concern to the man. Find the question Jesus addressed to the blind men at Jericho.

It is clear that when multitudes followed him it was because effective points of contact had already been established. Such was the case with the crowds to whom the Sermon on the Mount, or the Teaching on the Hill, as it might be called, was given. The two main general methods by which he himself had established such contacts are suggested in Luke 6: 17. What are these? But in the gathering of a crowd there is another influence at work. What is it? Find it in Matt. 4: 24. Putting these three things together, we see the crowds assembled because of what Jesus had said and done and because of social suggestion—the spreading of fame.

Both Matthew and Luke agree that Jesus began the teaching on the hill with the beatitudes, or characteristics of the blessed life. How did he connect up in this way with something astir in his hearers' own minds?

On another occasion, when teaching a multitude as it stood on the beach and he sat in a boat on the lake, he utilized the parable as the opening point of contact, beginning with that of the Sower. How would the parable appeal to something already in the minds of his hearers? Would they be more interested in the blessed life or in a story? See Matt. 13. Which appeals to the higher intelligence? Why did Jesus begin his teaching of multitudes with simple statements and then pass later to figurative language? This last question may have to wait till we make a special study of the parables. How did multitudes of people affect Jesus? See Matt. 9: 36 and 15: 32.

Jesus would eat and drink with publicans and sinners. His disciples did the same. This scandalized the Pharisees and their scribes. Why did Jesus do it? See Matt. 9: 10–13. What effect did such social freedom have on the Levis and the Magdalens? Would it be going too far to say Jesus was, as we say, "a good mixer"? Does being a good mixer necessitate doing wrong things? Jesus remarked that it was said of him, "Behold, a gluttonous man and a wine-bibber." Why is eating and drinking with a person such an intimate form of contact?

How did Jesus establish contact with Zaccheus? Read Luke 19: 1–10 with this question in mind. How did Jesus meet Zaccheus more than half way? Would you say that the habitual attitude of Jesus toward people was exclusive or democratic? Back of every contact established seems to have been the helpful disposition of Jesus, coupled with the desire to complete the fragmentary lives of people. How does the incident of Zaccheus show the use Jesus made of the occasion as it arose? This is so important a matter that we must give especial attention to it later.

In the triumphal entry, by riding upon a colt, the foal of an ass, with what possible content in the minds of the people was Jesus seeking connection? Read Matt. 21: 1–11; Mark 11: 1–11; Luke 19: 29–44; John 12: 12–19. Did he succeed? Here an act is used to make an appeal.

After the denial by Peter, how did Jesus reestablish contact with him? See Luke 22: 61. You notice the repeated references to the use of his eyes by Jesus. What others can you recall? The resurrection angel sent a special message to Peter. Mark 16: 7. How did Jesus himself reopen contact with Peter? See John 21: 15.

It would be worth while to follow this study with a careful account of the spirit contacts Jesus made after the resurrection with Mary Magdalene in the garden, with Cleopas and John on the way to Emmaus, with the other disciples, and with Thomas.

Sum up now the main modes of contact made by Jesus. How many have you? After all, just which ones are not open to us? All we require is the will and the skill.

When we reach "Apperception" we shall find it a way of keeping up the mental contact already made. See Patterson Du Bois, "The Point of Contact in Teaching."

CHAPTER V

HIS AIMS

A real teacher must have both strategy and tactics, that is, he must have both objectives and means for attaining them. Without strategy, tactics have no goal; without tactics, strategy has no means of attainment.

What were the objectives of the Great Teacher?

First, make a list of these for yourself, and then compare it with the one given below.

1. To do his Father's will and work. "My meat is to do the will of him that sent me and to accomplish his work" (John 4: 34).

2. To be accepted as the Messiah, "I that speak unto thee am he." "Whom say ye that I am?"

3. To win learners and to train them as witnesses of his. So he called many, and chose a few to be apostles, and sent them forth two by two, and said to them: "Ye are my witnesses."

4. To substitute vital for formal religion. This covers a great deal, including the prayer of the publican, the benevolence of the poor widow, fasting in secret, the elimination of the motives of murder and lust and hatred, perhaps even the destruction of the sacrificial system in the cleansing of the temple. "I desire mercy and not sacrifice." "Pray to thy Father in secret."

5. To fulfil the law in the new universal kingdom of social righteousness. "Think not that I am come to de-

stroy the law or the prophets. I am not come to destroy but to fulfil." Most of the parables were designed to make plain to discerning minds the nature of the Kingdom.

6. To show by example and to teach by precept the way of life. "I am come that they might have life, and that they might have it more abundantly." Through seeking and saving the lost, he would prevent the ultimate miscarriage of life. He came to bear witness to the truth that by losing life we gain it. He gave his life as a ransom for many.

7. To quicken the faith and hope of men. He added to John the Baptist's gospel of repentance the injunction: "Believe the gospel," that is, accept as true the good news of God's love and act accordingly. His concern was that at his coming again he should find faith on the earth.

8. To break the bonds of race prejudice. He talked with a Samaritan woman at high noon. He made a Samaritan the model neighbor of one of his stories. He healed the daughter of a Syrophœnician woman and the servant of a Roman centurion. He received Greeks and spoke to them of life through death, as Plato had done over three hundred years before. He talked of his "other sheep," of the leavening of "the whole," of the salt of "the earth," of the light of the "world."

9. To destroy the works of darkness. Thus by the finger of God he cast out demons, healed diseases, and relieved affliction of every kind, and gave his disciples power and authority over the demons.

How would you extend this list?

Note we have here read his aims in terms of his accomplishments. Is this justifiable? If so, why? If not, what were his aims in distinction from his accomplishments?

Which of these aims are practicable for his followers today?

In his aims as a teacher did Jesus place primary emphasis on the acting or the thinking of his pupils?

The statement of aims given above is drawn from his own teachings. Suppose we approach the matter from another angle. If you are somewhat familiar with modern educational thought, make a list of the aims of education as a present-day thinker might formulate them. Then consider the extent to which these aims appear in the deeds and words of Jesus. Such a mode of procedure would apply a modern standard, the highest we have, to his work done nearly twenty centuries ago.

The aims of education:

1. To develop a sound body.
2. To form a good character.
3. To refine feeling.
4. To inform and equip the intellect.
5. To make a good citizen.
6. To cultivate productive skill.
7. To relate life to its Source and Goal.

It is true that such a statement as this is synthetic. It probably would not be found in its entirety in the usual books today on educational theory. Points three and seven are very commonly omitted. But it is a fair composite picture of what educators hold today concerning the aims of education.

Now ask yourself the question: To what extent do these aims appear in the work of Jesus as teacher?

1. He healed the bodies of men and made them whole.

2. He lived and taught the highest standards of moral character.

3. He pointed out the beauties of nature.

4. He taught ethical and spiritual truths and trained the intelligence of his disciples.

5. He was a good citizen and taught obedience to civil authority.

6. He was a carpenter and taught the economic virtues.

7. He was the Son and spiritualized life.

We note then that Jesus practiced what modern educators preach, that complete education is sevenfold—namely, physical, moral, esthetic, intellectual, social, vocational, and spiritual. In both practice and theory the Master Teacher long ago set up the standards which are also those of our modern pedagogy.

What comments have you to make upon this showing?

G. Stanley Hall thinks that the great objective of Jesus was to bring men to attain, or at least to approximate, his own state of mind; that it was this objective which led him to become a teacher; that the difficulty of his task determined his methods of training a few, of reticence, and of healing. So men would be brought to recognize him for what he was without his open avowal of divine sonship, which some would regard as blasphemous and others as insane talk. And all this he was thinking through at the time of the Temptation.

"But now his thought must turn to the world of other men. What could be done with this great new insight so hard to grasp, so impossible to teach directly? . . . Thus he must probably always teach with reservations and with more or less veiled reticence, for to reveal all he had seen would spoil all. He must follow a program or curriculum, and must be a great teacher, for if others ever were to attain his state of mind or to get near it, and profit in proportion, it would never be by his method, viz., that of solitude, meditation, and prayer, but by objective demonstration. . . . A man conscious of his own essential divinity must give proof in object lesson form of his superiority over others whose souls had not realized their own consubstantiality with God."[1]

What do you think of Hall's views?

Would you say that one of the aims of Jesus was to establish religion as an ecclesiastical institution on the earth?

Did Jesus intend to reform Judaism or to found Christianity?

Review his aims and ask in which he succeeded best.

To what extent should his aims be ours?

[1] G. Stanley Hall, "Jesus, the Christ, in the Light of Psychology," Vol. I, p. 304.

CHAPTER VI

HIS USE OF PROBLEMS

What is a problem? Your answer?

When we stand at a fork in the road, we face a problem; that is, in case we are going somewhere and the road is new to us. In such a case our intellectual processes of reflection and deliberation are aroused, leading to a solution of the problem, upon the basis of which we may proceed on our journey.

The Greek original of the term suggests that a problem is something *cast before* the mind. Being there, it requires solution, if a solution can be had. This term is worth studying in the dictionary.

How many kinds of problems are there?

Some problems grow immediately out of our experience and their solutions affect daily conduct. These problems are *practical* in character. Other problems are proposed by the intellect to itself, their solutions are difficult or impossible to reach, and, if reached, they affect life little or none. These problems are *theoretical*.

Will this distinction between practical and theoretical problems hold? Only in a crude way. A man, let us say, does something wrong, and suffers remorse. He may wonder whether he could have done differently. He faces the problem of free will and determination. These are the forks in his road. Is his problem practical or theoretical? We may say practical in the sense that it grows out of his experience and his answer affects his conduct.

We may say theoretical in the sense that he is not sure of his answer, which he accepts, not proves.

Can you think of other problems difficult of classification?

How would you classify the problem of life after death? of the existence of God? of spirit communication? of reducing the high cost of living? of increasing the hire of teachers and preachers? of the habitation of Mars? of the Einstein theory of light? of leaky radiators? of the ouija board?

In sum, we may say, there are problems whose solutions affect the conduct of life, these are practical; there are problems whose solutions do not affect the conduct of life, these are theoretical; and there are problems, like free will, whose solutions are theoretical but whose applications are practical.

Can you see any relationship between the third group of problems and faith? We might say that faith is acting as though a theory were true.

It is also to be observed that the solution of a theoretical problem may in unexpected ways become practical, as when wireless telegraphy helps save life at sea. This is one justification for laboratories of pure research. Another, perhaps, is that knowledge is worth having for its own sake, even if no use can ever be made of it. Is this true?

So, the facing of a problem is the beginning of real thinking. Without a felt difficulty, thinking is only simulated. To think is to think *about*. And the thing really thought about is the problem. Dewey says[1]: "The need of clearing up confusion, of straightening out an

---

[1] Art. "Problem," in Monroe's "Encyclopædia of Education."

ambiguity, of overcoming an obstacle, of covering the gap between things as they are and as they may be when transformed, is, in germ, a problem."

May a problem be present in a situation without being recognized?

Is it a problem in teaching to find the problem?

Is it worth while to find the problem first?

Is what the teacher selects as the problem necessarily the same as the pupil's problem?

May the pupil have a problem of which he is not aware?

Does the setting of a task necessarily constitute a problem? What does? Dewey says: "As a matter of fact, the conditions in experience, the content, determine whether a matter is or is not a problem and what sort of a problem it is."

If facing a felt problem is the beginning of real thinking, it is also the basis of real teaching. Such teaching is not only interesting, it is also effective in changing conduct, and this is what we want in teaching morality and religion, which, if they do not affect life, are nothing.

Did Jesus use the problem method? Graves[2] devotes two pages to "His Use of the Problem with the Disciples," and says: "Like all great teachers, Jesus felt that real thinking begins with a problem."

Can you show the truth of this statement?

Can you distinguish between those problems sensed as such by his pupils and critics and those he brought to their attention? In the latter case they may not have been conscious of their problem until he spoke of it. In which group is Peter's question: "What shall we have?"

1 "What Did Jesus Teach?" p. 51, N. Y., 1919.

In which group is the teaching of Jesus: "How hardly shall they that have riches enter the kingdom of heaven"? Were the difficulties raised by his critics real problems?

Shall we say that every person requesting a blessing from Jesus brought a problem with him? Have you a case in mind in which Jesus sensed a deeper problem that was brought? (See Mark 2: 1-12.)

Have you a case in mind in which Jesus declined to deal with the problem brought? In this connection recall the request: "Speak to my brother that he divide the inheritance with me." Recall also how he reacted to their desire to make him king.

To realize whether Jesus used the problem method or not, make a list of persons he taught with their problems. To shorten it, you might omit the cases of healing on request, and you might utilize Mark's gospel, as the oldest and the shortest.

After making your list, compare it with the following one:

Persons	*Their Problems*
The scribes, Mark 2: 7.	Who can forgive sins?
Scribes and Pharisees, Mark 2: 16.	The association of Jesus with publicans and sinners.
"They," Mark 2: 18.	Why the disciples did not fast.
The Pharisees, Mark 2: 24.	Sabbath observance.
The scribes, Mark 3: 22.	How Jesus cast out demons (note their solution).
His fellow-townsmen, Mark 6: 2, 3.	The sources of Jesus' power.

Persons	*Their Problems*
The scribes and Pharisees, Mark 7: 5.	Why the disciples did not observe the traditions.
The Pharisees, Mark 8: 11.	They wanted a sign.
Peter, James, and John, Mark 9: 11.	The coming of Elijah.
The disciples, Mark 9: 34.	"Who is the greatest?"
John and others, Mark 9: 38.	Tolerance of other workers.
The Pharisees, Mark 10: 2.	Divorce.
The rich young ruler, Mark 10: 17.	Inheriting eternal life.
James and John, Mark 10: 37.	Sitting on his right and left hand.
Chief priests, scribes, and elders, Mark 11: 28.	The authority of Jesus.
Pharisees and Herodians, Mark 12: 14.	The tribute to Cæsar.
Sadducees, Mark 12: 23.	The resurrection.
A scribe, Mark 12: 29.	The first commandment.
Peter, James, John, and Andrew, Mark 13: 4.	"When shall these things be?"
Some at Simon's dinner, Mark 14: 4.	The waste of ointment.
The high priest, Mark 14: 61.	Whether Jesus claimed to be the Christ.

Doubtless, other incidents in Mark's gospel that contain certain problems could be cited.

Note that the problems faced here by Jesus were mostly not of his own choosing, but were brought to him, sensed as primary by those who brought them. Of three, however, he chose to make an issue, namely, the charge that he had Beelzebub, the indignation at the waste of the ointment, and the conversation of the disciples concerning the greatest.

This study might be carried through the other gospels. For example, how would you formulate the problem in the mind of Nicodemus as he came to Jesus by night? What were the problems of the Woman of Samaria?

Run again through the list given above and note what solution Jesus gave to each problem.

Run through it still again and note the effects on conduct of the solution given in each case when recorded.

The teaching of Jesus shows: problem—solution—action. Shall we regard these three as natural elements of every teaching act?

From the Sermon on the Mount make a list of problems upon which Jesus chose to speak, sensing them as the problems of the multitudes. To what extent, do you suppose, were these problems felt as such by the crowds themselves?

How would you classify the problems upon which Jesus spoke, as practical or theoretical? Which, if any, are theoretical?

Did Jesus sense the real needs of men better than they did themselves?

If Jesus had been a teacher of science and philosophy, would he have discussed theoretical problems more?

What may we as teachers of morality and religion learn from Jesus' use of the problem method?

To what extent does the teaching we know conform to this method?

What would happen if teachers and preachers began with problems?

Reshape next Sunday's Bible school lesson about a problem.

There is another mode of approach to this matter. The term problem suggests particularly something intellectual, though, of course, problems may be emotional and moral as well as intellectual. The word *need* suggests particularly what is felt as a need.

Make a list of as many of the needs of people as you can which Jesus met.

Compare your list with the following:

The healing of the body.

The forgiveness of sin.

The release from fear.

The satisfaction of the desire to know.

The redirection of motive.

Relief from Sabbatarianism.

Guidance in how to pray.

The right valuation of sacrifice and mercy.

Social recognition.

A universal rule of conduct.

A true estimate of wealth.

The dignity of humble service.

Right regard for children.

Ability to be cheerful in a world of tribulation.

Knowledge of the greatest commandment.

The right attitude toward the letter of Scripture.

The increase of faith.

The spirit of truth.

The resolution of doubt.

The showing forth of the Father.

The condemnation of hypocrisy in religion.

Ministry to cities and multitudes.

The restoration of religious sanity to diseased minds.

The satisfaction of hunger.

The welcome of sinners.

Is there any limit to a list of the needs of men met by Jesus? (Once a group provided me with a list of ninety-four such different needs.)

Could you illustrate from the gospels each of these needs?

Can you think of any moral or religious need of man not met by Jesus?

Are there needs of men in science, philosophy, art, production, manufacture, commerce, transportation, and politics, not met by Jesus? In what sense? Would an affirmative answer constitute an unworthy limitation on the influence of Jesus?

To be concrete, may a business man learn all he needs to know about the psychology of advertising from the gospels?

Perhaps we must distinguish between the inspiration to all that is good and needful, which we do find in Jesus, and the attainment of all such useful information, which, of course, we do not find in his recorded words. A Christian may study Greek tragedy, but his Christianity does not tell him what to think of Greek tragedy as a form of art.

We conclude, then, that Jesus met the moral and religious needs of men, and inspired them to find satisfaction of all their needs in the abundant life.

What difference would it make in our work if we met men on the ground of their problems and needs?

CHAPTER VII

HIS CONVERSATIONS

Washington Gladden has an essay entitled "Qualities of Good Conversation." Let me provide you with a brief summary of it, in the light of which we can study the conversations of Jesus.

QUALITIES OF GOOD CONVERSATION

"In politics, in religion, in the arts of life, opinions are oftener changed by familiar talk than by formal speeches. . . . But conversation is not merely a useful art, it is a fine art.

"There are just two indispensable qualifications of a good conversationalist. The first is a good mind, the second is a good heart. The good heart is by far the more important and the one more likely to be disregarded.

"The good mind implies: (1) Natural ability; (2) intelligence; (3) discipline.

"The good heart implies: (1) Good humor; (2) charitableness; (3) candor; (4) sympathy; (5) earnestness; (6) sincerity; (7) modesty.

"The good conversationalist is one who can not only talk well, but also listen well.

"I remember now the words of One whose conversations (for he never made speeches) have been the most precious legacy of the world for many centuries: 'How can ye, being evil, speak good things? for out of the abundance of the heart the mouth speaketh. A good man out of the good treasure of the heart bringeth forth good things: and an evil man out of the evil treasure bringeth forth evil things.' Here we come to the root of the matter. If you would talk well you must live well."

Let us now apply the findings of Dr. Gladden to the conversations of Jesus.

Do they reveal the good mind? and the good heart? Is there natural ability? intelligence? discipline of mind? good humor? charitableness? candor? sympathy? earnestness? sincerity? modesty?

How would you illustrate each of these characteristics by the conversations of Jesus?

How is the fact that he finally silenced his intellectual critics related to the quality of his mind?

How is the fact that Mary sat with joy at his feet related to the quality of both mind and heart?

How is the fact that he was untrained in the rabbinical schools of the time, yet was able to engage successfully in dialectic with their graduates, related to his natural ability?

How does the conversation concerning the fall of Siloam's tower reveal intelligence?

How does the conversation concerning the baptism of John reveal a well-disciplined mind?

How does the conversation concerning Herod's designs on his life show good humor?

What conversation reveals his charitableness? Was he uncharitable in his conversation with the Pharisees concerning *Corban*, or only just?

How is his candor revealed in his conversation with Pilate concerning kingship?

How is sympathetic insight shown in his conversation with Martha concerning domestic duties?

Did he ever descend from earnestness to flippancy? How are Peter's words, "Thou hast the words of eternal life," related to the quality of earnestness in Jesus?

How does sincerity appear in his conversation with the rich young ruler concerning inheriting eternal life? Have you further illustrations of sincerity? How do you interpret John 7:8?

How does modesty appear in the conversations of Jesus? Is it in the reply, "Why callest thou me good?" What other translation of this passage is there? Is this trait inconsistent with the self-assertion of Jesus?

Are there still other qualities of the good conversationist? How about fluency? brilliancy? wit?

Did Jesus exemplify any of these? Is there caustic wit in his conversation with the Pharisees concerning casting out demons: "And if I by Beelzebub cast out demons, by whom do your sons cast them out?" (Luke 11:19.)

Was Jesus a good listener? How could you show it?

Do you agree with the parenthetic remark of Dr. Gladden that Jesus "never made speeches"?

Almost any book of polite literature dealing with the art of conversation will include such hints as these: Don't use slang; avoid exaggeration; be genial; think before you speak; don't pun; don't argue; exclude religion and politics as topics; conceal temper; don't interrupt the speaker; adapt your conversation to your company; don't correct another in public.

To begin with, did Jesus frequent "polite" society?

Are such conversations recorded? How do the conversations as recorded differ in purpose from those of polite society?

In the days of Socrates, Plato, and Aristotle, men conversed on all the deep interests of life both in public places and in private homes. The results of these conversations were recorded and have since instructed the learned world. How do the conversations of Jesus with his disciples compare with these?

In the list of eleven hints given above, check the ones you think Jesus exemplified. Could you prove your points? Do any figures of speech of Jesus involve exaggeration? Did he ever pun? Did he argue? Did he discuss religion and politics? Did he at times show feeling in conversation? Have you a clear case where he interrupted a speaker? Did he ever correct the views of others in public? If Jesus had engaged only in polite conversations at such social functions as he attended, should we ever have heard of him? What kind of a guest was he?

Who are a few of the remembered talkers of the race? Why are they remembered?

Are there still some characteristics of the conversations of Jesus not yet mentioned? Reread Mark 10, 11, and 12 with this question in mind.

Shall we say that the conversations of Jesus were:

1. Brief?
2. Purposeful?
3. Direct, pointed, not evasive?
4. Personal?
5. Making a difference to the interlocutor?

6. Instructive, communicative?
7. Accompanied by use of eyes (Mark 10: 27)?
8. Responsive?
9. Courageous?
10. Rebuking?
11. Marvelous? (Mark 12: 17.)
12. Friendly?
13. Appreciative? (Mark 12: 34.)
14. Pleasure and pain-giving? (Mark 12: 37; 10: 22.)
15. Monologue or dialogue? Give and take?
16. Quick-witted?
17. Uncompromising?
18. Dignified?
19. Friend and enemy-making? (Mark 12: 12.)
20. Stimulating?

Take any one of the conversations of Jesus and find as many qualities in it as you can.

While no one wants always to be teaching people things, to what extent do you feel we are really utilizing to the full our conversations?

Did Jesus "talk shop"?

"When in Rome, do as the Romans do." Did Jesus?

Read carefully the following estimate and note any points of disagreement:

"This sense of humor made the common people hear him gladly. The stupidity and *faux pas* of the disciples, who understood him as little as Goethe's Wagner understood Faust; the address to the soul, 'Thou hast much goods laid up,' which suggests Holbein's 'Dance of Death'; the admonition not to sit in the chief seat at a feast, or ask to dinner only those who will ask you to dine in return; these and the many pithy epigrammatic sayings that the world knows by heart show that Jesus was a great conversationalist, as witty as he was wise; that he was as ready with pleasantry, satire, ridicule, and irony as he was with invectives."[1]

[1] G. S. Hall, "Jesus, the Christ, in the Light of Psychology," Vol. II, p. 421.

CHAPTER VIII

HIS QUESTIONS

Somehow at the beginning of this inquiry I sense that we are near the heart of the teaching methods of Jesus.

Recall now as many questions asked by Jesus as you can.

What are some of them?

The four gospels record over one hundred different ones.

Here are some of them:

"How is it that ye sought me?"

"Knew ye not that I must be in my Father's house?" (His first recorded words.)—Luke 2: 49.

"What seek ye?"—John 1: 38.

"Woman, what have I to do with thee?"—John 2: 4.

"Art thou the teacher of Israel, and understandest not these things?"—John 3: 10.

"If I told you earthly things and ye believe not, how shall ye believe if I tell you heavenly things?"—John 3: 12.

"Say not ye, There are yet four months, and then cometh the harvest"?—John 4: 35.

"Why reason ye in your hearts? Which is easier to say, Thy sins are forgiven thee; or to say, Arise and walk?" —Luke 5: 22, 23.

"Wherefore think ye evil in your hearts?"—Matt. 9: 4.

"Wouldst thou be made whole?"—John 5: 6.

"How can ye believe, who receive glory one of another,

and the glory that cometh from the only God ye seek not?"—John 5: 44.

"But if ye believe not his writings, how shall ye believe my words?"—John 5: 47.

"Did ye never read what David did?"—Mark 2: 25, 26.

"Or, have ye not read in the law?"—Matt. 12: 5.

"Is it lawful on the sabbath day to do good, or to do harm? to save a life, or to kill?"—Mark 3: 4.

"What man shall there be of you, that shall have one sheep?" etc.—Matt. 12: 11.

"But if the salt have lost its savor, wherewith shall it be salted?"—Matt. 5: 13.

"For if ye love them that love you, what reward have ye?"—Matt. 5: 46, 47.

"Is not the life more than the food?"

"Are not ye of much more value than they?"—Matt. 6: 25, 26.

"And which of you by being anxious can add one cubit to his stature?"

"And why are ye anxious concerning raiment?"—Matt. 6: 27, 28.

"Shall he not much more clothe you?"—Matt. 6: 30.

"And why beholdest thou the mote that is in thy brother's eye?" etc.—Matt. 7: 3, 4.

"Or what man is there of you, who, if his son shall ask him for a loaf will give him a stone?"—Matt. 7: 11.

"Do men gather grapes of thorns?"—Matt. 7: 16.

"What went ye out into the wilderness to see?"—Matt. 11: 7–9.

"But whereunto shall I liken this generation?"—Matt 11: 16.

"Which of them therefore will love him most?"—Luke 7: 42.

"Seest thou this woman?"—Luke 7: 44.

"How can Satan cast out Satan?"—Mark 3: 23.

"And if I by Beelzebub cast out demons, by whom do your sons cast them out?"—Matt. 12: 27.

"Or how can one enter into the house of the strong man, unless he first bind the strong man?"—Matt. 12: 29.

"Ye offspring of vipers, how can ye, being evil, speak good things?"—Matt. 12: 34.

"Who is my mother?"—Matt. 12: 48.

This list is drawn from approximately the first third of the ministry of Jesus. Would it not be worth your while to complete the list?

What are some of the general characteristics of the questions asked by Jesus? Answer for yourself first, and then read on.

"A leading question" is one the very form of which suggests the answer that is wanted. Did Jesus use the leading question?

Do you chance to know whether Socrates made use of leading questions? In honor of Socrates, questioning is called "the Socratic art."[1]

Is it better teaching to use or not to use the leading question?

Socrates regularly used a long series of leading questions to bring an idea to birth in the mind of his interlocutor. Did Jesus do this?

If you are interested in this topic, read Xenophon's

---

[1] For a comparison of Jesus and Socrates as questioners, see the writer's book on "Story Telling, Questioning, and Studying,' pp. 103–110.

"Memorabilia" and compare it with Mark, and Plato's "Phaedo" and compare it with John. As Mark and John are related to Jesus, so roughly are Xenophon and Plato related to Socrates. In each case we have a master teacher who spoke but did not write presented to us by two pupils, one prosaic and one poetic.

Take the following list of characteristics and find at least one question of Jesus illustrating it:

Original.

Practical.

Personal.

Rhetorical.

Stimulating.

Definite.

Searching.

Adapted to the individual.

Silencing.

Clear.

Brief.

How would you enlarge this list of the characteristics of the questions of Jesus?

Turn to the purpose of his questions. For what purposes did Jesus ask questions? Make your own list.

Find at least one question of Jesus used for each of the following purposes:

To make one think.

To secure information for himself (Luke 8: 30).

To express an emotion.

(What emotions are expressed? See John 3: 10; Luke 5: 22, 23; Matt. 12: 34.)

To introduce a story.

To follow up a story.

To recall the known (Mark 2: 25, 26).

To awaken conscience (Matt. 23: 17).

To elicit faith (Mark 8: 29).

To clarify the situation (Mark 10: 3).

To rebuke criticism (Mark 2: 25, 26).

To put one in a dilemma (Mark 3: 4).

Add to this list of purposes.

What are some of the psychological effects of the question?

For example, how does a good question affect intelligence? interest? attention? memory? even conduct? To what other psychological effects would you refer?

There were certain questions asked by Jesus which his critics were unable or unwilling to answer. Can you recall some?

Among these were the following:

"Is it lawful on the sabbath to do good, or to do harm? to save a life or to destroy it? But they held their peace" (Luke 6: 9).

"Which of you shall have an ass or an ox fallen into a well, and will not straightway draw him up on a sabbath day? And they could not answer again unto these things" (Luke 14: 5, 6).

"The baptism of John, whence was it, from heaven or from men? . . . And they answered Jesus, and said, We cannot tell" (Matt. 21: 25–27).

"If David then calleth him Lord, how is he his son? And no one was able to answer him a word" (Matt. 22 45, 46).

Why did Jesus ask each of these questions?

Can you think of others he asked they did not answer?

Why did they not answer in each case?

If they were unable to answer, why did not Jesus answer for them? Pay particular attention to this question. Study Luke 22: 67.

How would you answer each of the questions the Jews did not answer—especially the one concerning David's son?

With what manner do you picture Jesus asking questions?

Earnest?

Sympathetic?

Inquisitorial?

Deliberate?

Reproving?

Spontaneous?

Any other manner?

Cite at least one question illustrating each of your answers.

Do you think Jesus ever prepared any question in advance of using it? For example, that concerning the baptism of John, or the Christ as the son of David.

There was at least one question Jesus asked of God. What was it? See Mark 15: 34.

How do you interpret this question?

What is its answer?

Does the twenty-second psalm, from which it is a quotation, throw any light on the answer?

Jesus petitioned God for many things—did he ever ask any other question of God?

From this study do you get the impression that the

atmosphere of Jesus was lethargic, or charged with intellectual inquiry?

Choosing between these two things, would you say that Jesus came to ask questions or to answer them? Of course he came to do both, and did both, and many other things besides, but which of these two did he do mainly?

Read the following quotation from Dr. Merrill, and see if you agree with him:

"His aim, as the Great Teacher of men, was, and ever is, not to relieve the reason and conscience of mankind, not to lighten the burden of thought and study, but rather to increase that burden, to make men more conscientious, more eager, more active in mind and moral sense.

"That is to say, He came not to answer questions, but to ask them; not to settle men's souls, but to provoke them; not to save men from problems, but to save them from their indolence; not to make life easier, but to make it more educative. We are quite in error when we think of Christ as coming to give us a key to life's difficult textbook. He came to give us a finer textbook, calling for keener study, and deeper devotion, and more intelligent and persistent reasoning."[2]

One of the reputed sayings of Jesus is: "They who question shall reign." Do you think it sounds like him? Or is it too consciously pedagogic or philosophic, as were the Greeks?

Francis Bacon said: "The skilful question is the half of knowledge." Would you agree? Can the skilful question be asked without knowledge?

---

[2] W. P. Merrill, "Christian Internationalism," pp. 42, 43.

What would be a good badge of the teacher's profession?

What other phase of the topic, "Jesus as Questioner," would you like to consider?

How may we become better questioners?

CHAPTER IX

HIS ANSWERS

Suppose you were going to present this topic, how would you do it?

Should teachers be as ready to answer questions as to ask them?

What if they don't know the answer?

Which is the more natural situation, when pupils or teachers ask the questions?

When are questions irrelevant or out of order?

What should the answer to such be?

As we studied the earlier part of the ministry for Jesus' questions, we will study the latter part for his answers, so as not to duplicate material.

First, study for yourself a few of the answers he gave. Note their characteristics. Find them in Matt. 22, Mark 12, and Luke 20.

Let us study some of his answers. After speaking his first parable concerning the four kinds of soils, his disciples asked, "Why do you speak in parables?" See his long, full answer in Matt. 13: 10–23. What is his answer in brief? Was it satisfactory to the disciples? Is it to you?

Note also that even the disciples did not understand this parable. This seems to have surprised Jesus (Mark 4: 13). But at their request he explained its meaning. He made his meaning plain to those who desired it and he explained why he used "dark sayings" at all.

In the midst of the sudden storm that swept down on

the lake, they awoke him, saying, "Master, carest thou not that we perish?" First, he quieted the sea, and then asked, "Why are you afraid like this? Why not have faith?"

What is significant in his answer here?

At least three things stand out. First of all he answers the question of alarm by doing something. Then, after quiet was restored and their paroxysm of fear was past, he replied, not to their question, but to their real need with two other rhetorical questions, in which he rebuked their fearfulness and its cause—lack of faith. This question he answered with a deed, and themselves he answered by asking two more questions.

At the feast of Matthew Levi the Pharisees and their scribes murmured against his disciples, and asked: "Why eateth your Teacher with the publicans and sinners?" The reply of Jesus was: "They that are whole have no need of a physician, but they that are sick. But go ye and learn what this meaneth, I desire mercy and not sacrifice: for I came not to call the righteous but sinners" (Matt. 9:11-13).

Study this answer carefully. Note the figure of speech in the answer. Also the quotation from Hosea. Also the statement of his mission.

Is there any sarcasm in referring to the Pharisees as "whole" and not needing a physician?

Their question implied a criticism of his conduct. His reply justified his intimate association at table with tax-gatherers and sinners.

Some of the disciples of John asked him: "Why do we and the Pharisees fast oft, but thy disciples fast not?"

Jesus had the greatest respect for John and his disciples, though their viewpoints of the kingdom were antipodal. This question was not asked in criticism. John's disciples were honestly puzzled and wanted light. Jesus replied: "Can the sons of the bridechamber fast while the bridegroom is with them? as long as they have the bridegroom with them they cannot fast. But the days will come, when the bridegroom shall be taken away from them, and then will they fast in that day" (Mark 2: 19, 20).

What a beautiful figure of speech! Who was the bridegroom?

How gentle this reply! With all tenderness a full explanation is given why his disciples did not fast.

To that part of their question, "Why do we fast?" Jesus did not reply. Is there anything significant in this? Did Jesus want to avoid any criticism of John to his disciples?

Is there tact in this answer?

Why did he refer to the time when his disciples would fast?

In his answer he passes on to give the parable of the new wine and the new cloth. What is the bearing of this parable on the situation? Does it contain by implication the answer to the original first part of their question: "Why do we fast"? Note the delicacy of putting the implied criticism of John's system in a parable.

One of his disciples, Andrew, Simon Peter's brother, at the time of the feeding of the five thousand, said unto him: "There is a lad here, who hath five barley loaves and two fishes: but what are these among so many?"

(John 6: 9.) "And he said, Bring them hither to me" (Matt. 14: 18).

There is a wonderful meaning hidden in this answer to a hopeless question. Think it out.

The whole sixth chapter of John is a very mine for studying Jesus' answers to questions.

The Pharisees and the scribes asked him: "Why walk not thy disciples according to the tradition of the elders, but eat their bread with defiled hands?"

His reply was: "Well did Isaiah prophesy of you hypocrites, as it is written, This people honoreth me with their lips, but their heart is far from me. But in vain do they worship me, teaching as their doctrines the precepts of men. Ye leave the commandment of God, and hold fast the tradition of men." Then he passes on to speak of Corban and gives the parable concerning defilement. Read it all in Mark 7: 9–23.

Does Jesus speak to the Pharisees in the same spirit as to John's disciples? What is the difference? Why this difference?

Note he answers with a question, with a quotation from Isaiah, with an illustration of his charge, and with a parable. Does the fullness of this reply denote any exasperation with the Pharisees?

Compare this answer with that given the Pharisees and Sadducees on seeking a sign. See it in Matt. 16: 1–4. Again there is an illustration, a charge, and an Old Testament reference.

Coming down from the mount of transfiguration, the disciples asked him: "Why then say the scribes that Elijah must first come?" And he answered and said,

"Elijah indeed cometh, and shall restore all things: but I say unto you, that Elijah is come already, and they knew him not, but did unto him whatsoever they would. Even so shall the Son of man also suffer of them" (Matt. 17: 10-12).

This reply accepts a scribal teaching, but gives it a new interpretation. Did Jesus then believe in reincarnation? Who was this Elijah? Did John regard himself as Elijah? (See John 1: 21.) Note the readiness with which Jesus answers questions, even this one involving technical scribal exegesis. How do you explain this?

After his healing of the demoniac boy following the Transfiguration, the disciples came unto Jesus when he was come into the house, and asked him privately, "Why could not we cast it out?"

"And he saith unto them: Because of your little faith: for verily I say unto you, if ye have faith as a grain of mustard seed, ye shall say unto this mountain, Remove hence to yonder place; and it shall remove; and nothing shall be impossible unto you" (Matt. 17: 20). "This kind can come out by nothing, save by prayer" (Mark 9: 29).

What do you see in this answer?

What could Jesus have meant by "faith"?

Are his words to be taken literally? If so, has anyone ever had this faith? If not, what does the figure mean? What kind of a figure is it?

The answer connects faith and prayer. What is the connection in the practice of healing?

These illustrations of the answers of Jesus might be greatly extended. Let us take only one more very instructive one.

The Jews marveled at his teaching given in the temple at the feast of tabernacles, saying, "How knoweth this man letters, having never learned?" His reply was: "If any man willeth to do his will, he shall know of the teaching, whether it be of God, or whether I speak from myself." This was not all he said; see it in John 7: 17–19.

Was this an answer at all to the question? If so what is its meaning?

Find and study the replies of Jesus to the following questions:

"What then sayest thou of her?"

"Where is thy father?" (Was this intended as an insulting taunt?)

"How sayest thou, Ye shall be made free?"

"Say we not well that thou art a Samaritan and hast a devil?"

"Hast thou seen Abraham?"

"How oft shall my brother sin against me and I forgive him?"

"Wilt thou that we bid fire to come down from heaven, and consume them?"

"What shall I do to inherit eternal life?"

"Who is my neighbor?"

"Speakest thou this parable unto us, or even unto all?"

"Are they few that be saved?"

"Is it lawful for a man to put away his wife?"

"Why did Moses command to give a bill of divorcement?"

"What good thing shall I do that I may inherit eternal life?"

"What lack I yet?"

"Who then can be saved?"

"What then shall we have?"

"Dost thou not care that my sister did leave me to serve alone?"

"Who did sin, this man or his parents, that he should be born blind?" (Did the disciples then believe that a man's own sin might cause him to be born blind? How?)

"Who is he, Lord, that I may believe on him?"

"How long dost thou hold us in suspense?"

"Hearest thou what these are saying?"

"By what authority doest thou these things?"

"Is it lawful to give tribute unto Cæsar or not?"

"Whose wife shall she be?"

"Which is the great commandment in the law?"

"Where wilt thou that we make ready for thee to eat the passover?"

"Dost thou wash my feet?"

"Is it I?"

"How know we the way?"

"Answerest thou the high priest so?"

"Art thou the Christ?"

"Art thou the King of the Jews?"

"Speakest thou not unto me?"

"What shall this man do?"

"Dost thou at this time restore the kingdom to Israel?"

If you have difficulty in finding some of these questions, use a good concordance.

Ought we to know the gospels practically by heart?

How well do the Chinese scholars know Confucius?

Are you surprised at the number of questions asked of Jesus?

There are many not in the list given above. Can you add to it?

Before two questioners Jesus did not answer. Who were these? Why did he not answer in each case?

Jesus asked some questions that his critics could not answer. Did they ever ask him a question he could not answer?

Was the attitude of Jesus encouraging to questioners? (See John 16: 19.)

Did Jesus answer the questioner as well as the question? This is one of the most significant things about his answers. Illustrate from his answer to the Sadducees concerning the resurrection.

A good teacher is not only ready to answer, but he makes the most of the answers of his pupils. Did Jesus do this? In what instances? Recall such comments as: "In that saidst thou truly," and "Thou art not far from the kingdom of God."

It is time to sum up. Draw up a list of the main characteristics of the answers of Jesus.

Give at least one answer that illustrates each of the following characteristics:

Informational, i. e., his answer gave information.

Profound (for a series of ever profounder answers, see John 6).

An answer in the form of a question.

An answer in the form of a dilemma.

An answer to the questioner as well as the question.

A real but not obvious answer.   (See Luke 17: 37.)

An answer different from the one wanted.

An answer in the form of a story.

Silence in answer.

An indirect answer (see Matt. 18: 1–6).

A practical answer to an academic question (Luke 13: 23, 24).

Are there still other characteristics of his answers?

Was he ever caught "napping"?

One of the characteristics of genius is ever to be at one's physical and moral best. Was this true of Jesus?

One of my students once gave me the following outline in a report on "The Answers of Jesus." Read it with a view to agreeing or disagreeing with its views.

OUTLINE

1. He answered in good faith.

   He never laughed at a question.

   He never hedged, or dodged a vital question.

   He never answered, "I don't know."

2. His answer was dependent on the motive back of the question.

   He did not satisfy curiosity—"no sign shall be given."

   "By what authority doest thou these things?" "I also will ask you one question."

   Vital questions received a straight answer. Matt. 26: 63, 64.

3. They tended to lead to more thinking.

   Lead questions: "Whom do men say that I am?"

   "What is written in the law?"

4. His answers often called for action.

   "Where dwellest thou?" "Come and see."

   "What must I do to inherit?" "Sell, give, come, follow."

5. His answers contained concrete illustrations.

"Who is my neighbor?"   The Good Samaritan.

What do you think of this outline?

What may we learn in our own practice from the answers of Jesus?   Give some time to this question.

SOME REFERENCES ON HIS QUESTIONS AND ANSWERS

Barnard, P. M., Art. "Questions and Answers," in "Dictionary of Christ and the Gospels."

Denney, "Gospel Questions and Answers."

Knight, "The Master's Questions to His Disciples."

Horne, "Story-Telling, Questioning, and Studying."

CHAPTER X

HIS DISCOURSES

Under what circumstances is it proper for a teacher to lecture?

Think of the right answer to this question.

Is the lecturing that leaves the group passive and impressed justifiable?

Is it proper to lecture on material with which the group is already acquainted?

Is it best to lecture to a small and informal group?

To what extent can you give another man an idea?

"No impression without expression" is an educational principle. How would this principle affect lecturing?

If we could discuss these questions together, we might conclude that lecturing is justifiable when the lecturer has something new to say; when the group is large, too large for question and answer and for discussion; when the occasion is consequently somewhat formal. But in all these cases, if possible, the lecture should be followed by discussion and conference.

One is sometimes forced into lecturing because of the unpreparedness of the group, though small, to ask, to answer, or to discuss. If there are any such groups! Social habit in any community also has something to do with the passive or active attitude of the auditors.

Can you think of other circumstances under which one should lecture—e. g. when immediate information is demanded as a basis of judgment?

Did Jesus ever make use of the lecture method? Preaching is, of course, one form of this method. The difference probably between an academic lecture and a sermon is that the former appeals mainly to the intellect, while the latter appeals mainly to the emotions and the will; that is, the former communicates ideas and the latter awakens impulses.

Were the discourses of Jesus academic or practical in character?

It is easy to begin by thinking of the *places* where Jesus spoke his discourses.

Recall all you can now. Do this before you read on.

Among these places are: The mountain; the lakeside; the synagogue in Nazareth, also in Capernaum and in many other towns and cities; the Mount of Olives, from which the Lament over Jerusalem was uttered; Bethesda, in Jerusalem; private homes; the open country; and the Temple.

Can you add to this list?

In what place, if any, would Jesus be unwilling to speak?

Think next of the *occasions* of his discourses. What were some of these?

Among such occasions are: The sight of the multitudes; a question asked by one of the crowd, receiving a longer answer than usual; a criticism passed upon some wonderful work of healing done; the sending forth of the twelve, and also of the seventy; the calumny that he had a devil, requiring refutation; the synagogue service on the Sabbath day; the departure of the messengers of John; the charge that he cast out devils by the prince of devils; the demand for a sign; a question from the disciples, requiring a full answer, concerning, say, the meaning of one of the parables, though only disciples heard such explanations.

Add to this list of occasions when Jesus used the method of public discourse. You will have little difficulty in doing so.

Think about the *length* of these discourses. Which is the longest one recorded? Where may it be found? How many minutes would it require to read this entire utterance aloud in a deliberate manner? Why not do so and see? (Is it Matt. 5–7, or John 14–17?)

Do you get the impression that the evangelists give us the full discourse in each case or only portions? (See the remarkable statement in John 21: 25.) Are there instances of their referring to preaching journeys without stating his utterances? (See Matt. 4: 23.) Why do you suppose his discourses were not more fully recorded? Do you suppose that on different occasions Jesus spoke similarly on similar themes? Of course our answers to many questions must remain in the realm of opinion.

Do you think the report in Matthew of the Sermon on the Mount, taking about twenty minutes to read aloud deliberately, may be a condensation of what Jesus actually said at greater length? Or, may it contain parts of different discourses? For this last question compare Luke 6: 20–49 with Matt. 5: 3 to 7: 27, noting how much more material Matthew reports than Luke.

Some think that the spoken discourse of Jesus may have occupied a longer time through his addressing only those near him, say, as he sat on the mount, and these in turn passing back his words to the others. What do you think of this? Would it be a good method, psychologically?

To what *audiences* did Jesus speak publicly? Recall for yourself.

These audiences were differently composed at different times.

Regularly some of the twelve disciples were present, though what makes his discourse "public" is that others than the twelve disciples heard him at some length on a given theme. These others were at times some of his followers, the apostles; or more or less sympathetic men, women, and children from the neighboring towns or even countries; or at times hostile critics from Jerusalem; or assembled guests at a social dinner. His audiences thus were groups mixed in various ways, from the standpoints of social standing, sex, sympathy with him, and age.

How otherwise would you characterize his audiences?

Would you regard Jesus as a master of assemblies?

By the way, of what church was Jesus pastor? And to what denomination did he belong? Was he a member of the congregation of a Jewish synagogue? If so, where? Did he cease to be such? If so, when? What difference to us do the answers to such questions make?

Upon what *themes* did Jesus speak? Or, did he rather give expository sermons on Old Testament texts? Did he ever do the latter? (Cf. Luke 4: 16–22.)

Among his themes note the following:

The Meaning of the Parable of the Tares, Matt. 13: 36–52.

The Leaven of the Pharisees, Matt. 16: 5–12.

His Church, Matt. 16: 13–20.

His Coming Death, Matt. 16: 21–28.

His Coming Death (again), Matt. 17: 22, 23.

His Coming Death (still again), Matt. 20: 17–19.

Elijah's Having Come, Matt. 17: 9–13.

The Mission of the Seventy, Luke 10: 1–24.

Prayer, Luke 11: 1–13.

The Unjust Steward, Luke 16: 1–13.

Occasions of Stumbling, Luke 17: 1–4.

Unprofitable Servants, Luke 17: 5–10.

Faith, Matt. 21: 21, 22.

Humility, John 13: 12–20.

The Lord's Supper, Matt. 26: 26–29.

The Suffering of the Christ, Luke 24: 17–27.

The Preaching of Repentance, Luke 24: 36–49.

Feeding the Lambs and Sheep, John 21: 15–23.

The Great Commission, Matt. 28: 16–19.

The nineteen discourses listed above are short and were delivered to a portion of the Twelve, or to all the Twelve, or to these with still others of his followers present. These could not strictly be called "public" discourses, as outsiders did not hear them. Some of these discourses may have been longer than reported.

The following four discourses were delivered to the same chosen groups as above, but are reported at greater length:

The Mission of the Twelve, Matt. 10: 1–42.

True Greatness, the Sinning Brother, and Forgiveness —one complex discourse, Matt. 18.

The Second Coming, the Ten Virgins, the Talents, and the Last Judgment—one discourse, Matt. 24, 25. (Cf. "all these words," Matt. 26: 1.)

The Farewell Discourse and Prayer, John 14–17.   (Is this the longest recorded continuous utterance of Jesus?)

Upon the following eight themes he spoke to mixed audiences, apparently small, of disciples and others:

Fasting, Luke 5: 33–39.

Sabbath Observance, Matt. 12: 1–8.

Following Him, Luke 9: 57–62.

Eternal Life and the Good Samaritan, Luke 10: 25–37.

Divorce, Matt. 19: 3–12.

The Peril of Wealth, Matt. 19: 16–30.

The Laborers in the Vineyard, Matt. 20: 1–16.

His Death and Glory, John 12: 20–26.

Upon the following (how many?) themes he spoke briefly to mixed audiences, apparently large, of disciples and others:

Blasphemy, Matt. 12: 22–37.

Signs, Matt. 12: 38–45.

Signs (again), Matt. 16: 1–4.

Signs (still again), and Demons, Luke 11: 14–36.

Traditions, Matt. 15: 1–20.

Denunciation of the Pharisees, Covetousness, Trust, Watchfulness, the Faithful Steward, Division, and Interpreting the Time—one discourse, Luke 12.

Repentance, and the Barren Fig Tree, Luke 13: 1–9.

The Good Shepherd, John 10: 1–18.

His Messiahship, John 10: 22–38.

Sabbath Healing, the Mustard Seed, and Leaven, Luke 13: 10–21.

The Elect, Luke 13: 23–30.

The Lament over Jerusalem, Luke 13: 34, 35.

Counting the Cost, Luke 14: 25–35.

The Rich Man and Lazarus, Luke 16: 14–31.

The Coming of the Kingdom, Luke 17: 20–37.

Prayer, the Importunate Widow, the Pharisee and Publican, Luke 18: 1–14.

His Authority, Tribute to Cæsar, the Resurrection, the Great Commandment, the Son of David—public replies to critics in the Temple, Luke 20.

Belief and Unbelief, John 12: 44–50.

Upon the following themes he spoke at length to mixed audiences of disciples and others:

The New Kingdom, Matt. 5–7. ("The Sermon on the Mount.")

His Relations with the Father, John 5: 19–47.

John the Baptist, Matt. 11: 7–30.

The First Group of Parables, Matt. 13: 1–53.

The Second Group of Parables, Luke 15–17: 10.

The Bread of Life, John 6: 22–65.

His Mission, John 7–8.

Denunciation of the Pharisees, Matt. 23: 1–39. (Was this his last public discourse?)

Upon the following themes he spoke to others than the disciples, whose presence is not clearly implied:

Forgiveness, the Two Debtors, Luke 7: 36–50.

Tradition, Matt. 15: 1–20.

Denunciation of Pharisees and Lawyers, Luke 11: 37–54.

Modesty, Giving Feasts, the Great Supper, and Excuses, Luke 14: 1–24.

Salvation to Zacchæus, with Parable of the Pounds, Luke 19: 1–27.

Reviewing the main themes[1] upon which Jesus spoke,

---

[1] For these classifications of themes I am indebted to the article by E. C. Dorgan, in "Dictionary of Christ and the Gospels," on "Discourse."

what is your impression as to (1) their comprehensiveness; (2) their adaptation to the needs of his day? How many different themes do you estimate there are? Anticipate here the later question: What may we learn from the discourses of Jesus?

Recall also the many references to discourses of his with little or no mention of themes. (Cf. Matt. 4: 17; Matt. 4: 23, 24; Luke 5: 17; Luke 8: 1–3; Mark 6: 1–6; Matt. 9: 35–38; Matt. 11: 1; Luke 13: 10, 22; Mark 11: 17.)

To appreciate both the form and the content of the discourses of Jesus, take one of the longer ones, and make an *outline* of it, indicating the main points.

The following will serve as an example of such an outline. No two outlines made by different persons will be exactly alike. You will note here that in addition to the main points the outline provides an introduction and a conclusion from the record itself, and also introduces a summary not in the record. Note whether the outline is strengthened or weakened by these additions.

How would you modify this outline?

OUTLINE OF THE SERMON ON THE MOUNT

I. Introduction: the Multitudes, the Disciples, the Master, Matt. 4: 25, 5: 1, 2.

II. The Main Points:

A. Beginning: The nine Beatitudes: a new set of values, Matt. 5: 3–12.

B. Middle:

1. His disciples are salt and light, Matt. 5: 13–16.

2. Jesus fulfils the law and the prophets, Matt. 5: 17–48.—Five illustrations: Murder, adultery, oaths, retaliation, enemies.

3. Righteousness before God, not men, Matt. 6: 1–18.—Three illustrations: Almsgiving, prayer, fasting.

4. The true treasure is heavenly, Matt. 6: 19–24.

5. Anxiety not for disciples, Matt. 6: 25–34.

6. Judgment of others condemned, Matt. 7: 1–5.

7. Reverence for sacred things, Matt. 7: 6.

8. Seeking and finding, Matt. 7: 7–11.

9. The Golden Rule, Matt. 7: 12.

10. The two gates, Matt. 7: 13, 14.

11. Warning against false prophets, Matt. 7: 15–23.

C. Application: The two foundations, Matt. 7: 24–27.

III. Summary: Jesus sets forth the constitution of the Kingdom of Heaven.

IV. Ending: The multitudes are astonished and follow, Matt. 7: 28–8: 1.

A friend kindly provides me with this suggestion about condensing the several main points:

"Does it not naturally fall into two big heads? The first part of the material has to do with how Jesus' standard of morality is different from that current. 'Ye have heard' and 'I say unto you.' The second part deals with how Jesus' emphasis in religion was different. The Pharisees emphasized the trinity of virtues, almsgiving, prayer, and fasting, and criticized those who did not conform. Jesus insisted upon reality (doing things in secret), charity (judge not that ye be not judged), deeds (not every one that saith unto me).

"Might it not be better to classify this material of eleven points in a couple of big heads?"

What do you think of this suggestion?

Thinking over the whole range of the discourses of Jesus, how would you *characterize* them in a general way?

Are they interesting? profound? original? authoritative? serious? practical? formal? academic? convincing? persuasive? self-conscious? full of variety? monotonous? personal? direct? self-assertive? novel? thoughtful? searching? scientific? artistic? literary? social? moral? spiritual? entertaining? amusing? diverting? simple? uplifting? transforming? intellectual? emotional? truthful? gracious?

Check off in this list of possible characteristics the ones you regard as applicable to the discourses of Jesus. You may want to reread some of them before doing so.

In what *manner* do you picture Jesus as uttering these addresses? It is very difficult to say for sure, for the gospel writers do not portray the addresses of Jesus as a Greek or Roman rhetorician would surely have done. They say next to nothing about his manner. Our own answer must be mainly by means of the imagination.

In particular, as Jesus spoke, was he quiet? impassioned? dignified? enthusiastic? self-forgetful? sympathetic? sensitive to changes in his audience? choked at times with emotion? with or without gestures? with or without flushed countenance and flashing eyes as he denounced the Pharisees? tender? winning? with a natural tone of voice? thrilling?

How else would you describe his manner of presenting truth in discourse?

Do you feel it improper to try to realize the very speaking presence of Jesus in this way? If so, how would you account for this feeling? Would you justify it?

Turn to *the effects* of his discourses. How did they affect his disciples? the multitudes of common people? the religious leaders? the Nazareth synagogue congregation? those sent by the Pharisees to take him? Why did the common people hear him gladly? Why did his would-be captors testify: "Never man spake like this man"? (John 7: 46.) Why did great multitudes follow him after the Sermon on the Mount? What so amazed and angered the Nazareth group? Why were the Pharisees offended?

Can you recall still other effects of his discourses?

Jesus once said to the disciples who had asked him to explain the parable of the sower: "Know ye not this parable? and how shall ye know all parables?" (Mark 4: 13.) Does this suggest that he did or did not then have in mind other parables to speak? What does this suggest as to whether Jesus *prepared* himself in advance for some of his discourses? How are the eighteen silent years related to this question? Undoubtedly much that he said was uttered spontaneously out of a full soul. Does this apply to all he said? Recall his promise to the disciples that in the hour of persecution it should be given them what to say. If you concluded that for certain of his discourses Jesus had prepared himself in advance, would that, in your judgment, detract from him as a teacher?

A topic for investigation: Did Jesus discourse more or converse more? Which do the evangelists report more, his conversations or his sermons?

We are near the end of our review of this most fertile field of study. Finally, then, what may we learn from Jesus about discourse, lecture, or sermon? Write down as many answers as you can to this question. Look through the preceding material again with this thought in mind. If we, according to our poor ability, would imitate the Master Teacher in public address, what should we do?

What would be our preparation?

In what places would we be willing to speak?

Before what groups?

Under what circumstances?

Upon what great themes would we speak? Would these themes be problems near to or remote from the lives of those addressed?

Would we repeat the old or herald the new?

In what manner would we speak?

Would we be rather prophets or priests?

Would we trim the truth to suit?

Would we at times antagonize?

Would we "cry aloud and spare not"?

What else?

At the conclusion of one of these studies do you get the same impression as the author that there is a great deal more in these topics than we had thought in advance, and also a great deal more than we have thought yet?

Finally, thinking back over the past three chapters, did Jesus prefer to ask questions, to answer questions, or to use the discourse? How can we tell? Judging by the following quotation, what would Stanley Hall say?

"As one who loved to sharpen wits by dialogue and discussion in the sense in which Plato commends this method of investigation, and took pleasure in discourse with strangers, both men and women, although he preferred as a teacher to communicate his own and God's truth, he still took a true and pedagogic pleasure in answering questions and meeting objections."[2]

Do you agree with this view?

[2] G. S. Hall, "Jesus, the Christ, in the Light of Psychology," Vol. II, p. 423.

CHAPTER XI

HIS PARABLES

One of the most outstanding features of the method of Jesus as teacher is that he told stories. We call his stories parables, though some of his sayings regarded as parables are not exactly stories, but rather short comparisons, as "A city set on a hill cannot be hid" (Matt. 5: 14). There are some twenty-eight of these short comparisons and perhaps twenty-five different stories. About one fourth of all the spoken words of Jesus recorded by Mark are parables in this double sense of the term, and in Luke nearly half. The proportion is largest in Luke. The term "parable" occurs some fifty times in the New Testament.

Some things to do:

Read the four gospels and make a list of all the short comparisons you can find.

Make another list of the stories.

When you have done this, if you read German, turn to Jülicher, "*Die Gleichnisreden Jesu*," and compare your lists with his.

If you don't read German, turn to Stanley Hall (who follows Jülicher), "Jesus, the Christ, in the Light of Psychology," p. 517, and do the same.

What proportion of Matthew is occupied by parables?

What do you find peculiar about the form of the parable in John?

Why do you suppose Luke was so attracted by the parables?

What is the nature of a parable?

A parable is a comparison between familiar facts and spiritual truths. This comparison may be short and pithy, like "If the blind lead the blind, both shall fall into the ditch" (Matt. 15: 14), or it may be worked out in a story. If worked out in story form, the story may say one thing and mean another, as the story of the lost sheep found by the good shepherd, meaning lost man found by the Savior (Luke 15: 3-7). This is the true form of the parable, or the story may embody in itself the truth taught, without referring to another realm beyond itself, as the story of the Good Samaritan (Luke 10: 25-37). This form of the parable may be called an illustrative story. There is still a third form which the story may take. It is one in which the story and its meaning do not run parallel, like a man and his shadow, but the two are interwoven with each other, as in the story of the Good Shepherd (John 10: 1-21).

In summary:

1. Short comparisons, like the three-word shortest parable: "Physician, heal thyself" (Luke 4: 23).

2. A story suggesting a comparison between familiar facts and spiritual truths, like the story of the tares in the wheat. This is what people usually mean by a parable. Jesus told the story, but not its meaning, unless asked to do so privately by his disciples. It is this kind of parable which is familiarly referred to as "an earthly story with a heavenly meaning."

3. An illustrative story carrying the truth within itself,

not above itself, like the Pharisee and publican praying in the temple. One might call it a single-story story, not a double-story story, as the group above.

4. Allegory, in which the spiritual meaning of the story is woven into the telling of the story, as in the Vine and the Branches (John 15). Recall the question raised above as to the peculiar form the parable takes in John's gospel. Can you think of any explanation for this?

Now take your earlier list of the stories told by Jesus, and try to decide in the case of each story whether it is a true parable, or an illustrative story, or an allegory.

Which of the three groups is the largest?

In order to show very clearly the distinction between a true parable and an allegory, let me undertake the venturesome task of making a true parable based on the allegory of the Vine and the Branches.

First, read attentively John 15: 1–10.

Then read the following, which tries to separate out of the allegory the meaning from the story:

The Kingdom of Heaven is like unto a thrifty-looking vine planted by a vine-dresser, which turned out to be the wild plant of a strange vine, and failed to bring forth fruit. Then he planted a true vine, and cut away the branches that bore no fruit, and cast them forth, and they withered, and were gathered, and cast into the fire, and burned. But he pruned with his pruning-hook the fruitful branches remaining in the vine, that they might bear more fruit, and their fruit ripened, and gave joy to the vine-dresser.

And when he had ended, Simon Peter said unto him: "Master, declare unto us the parable."

And he said: Israel is the false vine, I am the true vine, and my Father is the vine-dresser. The word is

the pruning-hook, and ye are the branches—some fruitless, to be destroyed, because not continuing in me, and
some fruitful, to be saved, because continuing in me.
Abide in me, and I will abide in you.

What do you think of it?

What type of mind would prefer the allegory to the
parable?

Why not attempt the same with John 10: 1–5, and
with John 6: 30–40?

Since the teacher is concerned with the effects of his
teaching on the minds of his pupils, let us ask, What are
the mental *effects* of the parable? This will help us to
understand why Jesus made such large use of it

Try this experiment: Select one of the parables with
which you are least familiar, get some one to read it
aloud to you, and note carefully the mental effects upon
yourself. Or, you may select a friend capable of introspection, and do the same with him. Or, read the following parable carefully, and see what happens in your
own mind.

A certain teacher, noting that some of his pupils were
not making use of their opportunities, told his class this
story:

"Two men went into a shop of fine wares to buy. And
when they had made their purchases, the dealer wrapped
their parcels and laid them on the counter. Whereupon,
one of the two took up his parcel and departed to his
house, but the other left his parcel lying on the counter.
And the dealer said, 'See, you are leaving behind the
goods you purchased.' But he replied, 'Oh I didn't
mean to carry them away. I only came into your shop

for the pleasure of being with my companion, seeing, and buying, but not caring to take anything away with me.'"

Give this story a chance at you first, then write down some of its mental effects.

Some of the mental effects of the parable are: It holds attention through interest; it presents a mental challenge to discover the meaning (it is a kind of puzzle one wants to solve); there may be surprise at the turn the story takes (compare the stories of O. Henry); one's personal pride may be piqued; it may release effort of will if a personal application is made; and it is an aid to memory. It may give offense if one feels that there is an indirect personal thrust.

Compare now your list of effects with this list.

If you would really like to appreciate a parable, stop at this point, and write one yourself. This is proposed seriously, why not try?

Why did Jesus use parables?

Before reading further, turn to the following references, and try to answer the question for yourself: Matt. 13: 10–18; Matt. 13: 34, 35; Mark 4: 10–12; Mark 4: 33, 34; and Luke 8: 9, 10.

Now recall that the parables or "dark sayings" were spoken to a mixed company of enemies and friends, of persons typified by each of the four kinds of soil, and that they were explained privately to the disciples. They were spoken primarily to the indifferent and hostile public, but their spiritual meaning was interpreted only to earnest inquirers.

Why, then, were the parables used? To conceal truth

from the unreceptive and to reveal truth to the receptive
The parable was a way of separating the sheep from the
goats. It was the method whereby Jesus followed his
own injunction, and did not cast that which was holy
to the dogs, nor his pearls before swine. Had he done
so, they would have trampled them under foot (i. e.,
rejected his plain teaching) and turned again and rent
him (i. e., attacked the new prophet) sooner than they
finally did. The parable was the word which would judge
them at the last day, showing them not to belong to the
understanding kind. In repeating the injunction: "He
that hath ears to ear, let him hear," the line of distinction
is being drawn between those with and without the hearing ear. So that the result was, as the prophet had said,
for all their seeing they did not perceive, and for all their
hearing they did not understand, and so did not turn
and receive forgiveness (Matt. 13: 14, 15).

So Stanley Hall refers to the parables as "Binet tests of
spiritual insight." "Thus for genetic religious psychology
they serve as moron-finders."[1]

Very likely there are other reasons also why Jesus used
the parable. He adopted this method rather suddenly
in the midst of his public ministry when the tide of opposition was rising against him, perhaps as a mode of
self-protection in his teaching, enabling him to survive
until his time should come. Besides, the story is the
common Oriental method of imparting truth, and the
Old Testament prophets (see, for example, Ezekiel 17),
as well as the later Jewish rabbis, had used this method
though without the perfection of form displayed by Jesus.

---

[1] "Jesus, the Christ, in the Light of Psychology," p. 522.

Can you think of still other reasons why Jesus may have used the parable?

Stop at this point and see whether you are a "religious moron" or not. State the latent meaning of one of the more difficult parables, e. g., equal pay for unequal work (Matt. 20: 1–16).

How did the disciples themselves pass this test when they first heard the parables of the Sower and the Tares?

Briefly to repeat the kinds of parables, for a purpose:

Not all the sayings of Jesus that go by the name of "parables" belong in the same class. "Physician, heal thyself," and "If the blind lead the blind, both shall fall into the ditch," are very different from the story of the lost coin, or the lost sheep, or the lost son. These latter say one thing and mean another; they say something about the sense world and mean something about the spiritual world.   Both of these differ from the Good Samaritan or the Pharisee and the publican, which combine the spiritual and material worlds in one story. There is no parallelism, but the virtue is embodied in the story itself.

All three of these differ from the Good Shepherd, in which, as we have seen, the story and the meaning are closely interwoven, and the story is subordinate to the meaning in the telling. Perhaps this last should not be called a parable at all, but an allegory. What allegory did John Bunyan write?

The first kind of parables might be called proverbs, maxims, or aphorisms. The second class are properly called parables, because they convey a moral or religious truth in short-story form. The third are illustrative stories. And then, in the fourth place, we have the form that the parables take in John's gospel—the allegory.

Given these four headings, how would you *classify;*

"Ye cannot serve two masters."

"Take the lowest seat."

The Widow and the Unjust Judge.

The Ten Virgins.

The Tares and the Wheat.

The Foolish Rich Man.

Dives and Lazarus.

The Vine and the Branches.

The Bread of Life.

If you want an engaging hunt, classify all the sayings of Jesus you can find that belong under some one of the first three heads. There will be between fifty and seventy-five of them.

Now compare your findings with those of Jülicher ("*Die Gleichnisreden Jesu*"), followed by Hall ("Jesus, the Christ, in the Light of Psychology," p. 517).

But there is a yet more interesting mode of approach to the parables, because throwing more light upon the range and quality of the thinking of Jesus. Suppose we classify the parables according to the sphere from which they are drawn, whether things, plants, animals, or men. Some will be difficult to classify according to this principle, e. g., the drag-net with the fish, the sower with the seed and the soils, the lost coin with the woman seeking.

What we find on this basis is something like the following:

THINGS

The Salt of the Earth.

The Light of the World.
The City Set on a Hill.
The Light on a Candlestick.
Things That Defile.
Things Hidden and Revealed.
The Eye as the Light of the Body.
The New Cloth on the Old Garment.
The New Wine in the Old Bottles.
The House Divided against Itself.
The Two Houses Built on Rock and Sand.
The Four Soils.
The Drag-Net.
The Hid Treasure.
The Pearl of Great Price.
The Great Supper.

PLANTS

The Budding Fig-Tree.
The Tree "known by its fruits."
The Barren Fig-Tree.
The Seed Growing Independently.
The Mustard Seed.
The Tares and the Wheat.
The Leaven.

ANIMALS

The Carcass and the Eagles.
The Children's Meat and the Dogs.
The Lost Sheep.
The Sheep and the Goats.

HUMAN BEINGS

The Woman Seeking the Lost Coin.
The Servants Given the Talents.
The Servants Given the Pounds.
The Unprofitable Servants.
Children in the Market Place.
The Son Asking for a Fish or an Egg.
The Disciple and His Lord.
Blind Leaders.
The Two Masters.
The Scribe Instructed in the Kingdom.
The Thief in the Night.
The Ten Virgins.
"Physician, heal thyself."
The Whole Who Need No Physician.
No Fasting in the Bridegroom's Presence.
Counting the Cost of War or a Tower.
The Adversary in the Way.
Guests to Take the Lowest Seat.
The Neighbor in Need of a Loaf.
The Widow and the Unjust Judge.
The Unmerciful Servant.
He to Whom Much and Little Is Forgiven.
The Lost Son.
The Two Sons Commanded to Work.
The Defiant Tenants of the Vineyard.
The Unwilling Guests.
The Eleventh-Hour Man.
The Good Samaritan.
The Pharisee and the Publican.
The Foolish Rich Man.

Dives and Lazarus.

The Unrighteous Steward.

The Faithful Steward.

Servants Looking for Their Lord.

Where shall we put the parable of the unclean spirit wandering in desert places?

If these classifications will at all stand, they show that of a total of sixty-one different parables, sixteen or about twenty-six per cent deal with the inanimate world of things, while the remaining seventy-four per cent deal with the animate world of plants, animals, and men. Of these last, seven or about eleven and one half per cent of the total deal with plants; only four, or some seven per cent, deal with animals; while thirty-four, or over fifty-five per cent, deal with human relations.

THE PARABLES OF JESUS

	NUMBER	PER CENT
Things....................	16	26
Plants.....................	7	11.5
Animals..................	4	7
Human....................	34	55.5
	61	100

Stop here and consider what these results mean for the *quality* and *range* of the thinking of Jesus.

From these results it is very evident that the thinking of Jesus centered in the human world rather than in the world of animals, plants, and things. This gives a humanistic rather than realistic or scientific quality to his thinking. It is also clear from the relatively small place in his thinking of the inanimate world of things that his thinking was not static but dynamic in quality. The phenomena of growth rather than lifeless material especially affected his thinking. And from the great sweep of his illustrations from every department of creation it is clear that Jesus had a wide circle of interests; his thinking was comprehensive and not limited in range.

As pieces of literary composition, would you regard the parables as works of art? as models of the short-story form? Of course, Jesus only spoke them without writing them down, but he spoke them in such a way that they were easily remembered. Besides, he may have thought some of them out carefully in advance. Does not his question, already referred to, when the disciples asked him the meaning of the parable of the sower, perhaps his first parable: "Know ye not this parable? And how shall ye know all the parables?" indicate that he had some parables in mind which were not yet spoken?

Now any work of art embodies the ideal in some pleasing form of the real. The parable suggests the poetry of heaven by the prose of earth. It conveys a spiritual meaning by the aid of an earthly story. And this it does in a form pleasing to the imagination. It is proper, then, to regard the parable as a work of art. By the canons of literary criticism, the parable of the Prodigal Son is the world's greatest short story.

In what consists the *beauty* of the parable? Among the most beautiful of the parables are: The Lost Sheep, The Lost Son, The Hidden Treasure, and The Pearl of Great Price. Reread these at this point just to enjoy their beauty. Can you find them? If not, use the concordance. You will notice that the first two of these are parables of compassion, the other two are parables of value. Can you feel their beauty?

Now what are the elements of the parable that stir the esthetic sense within us, like a lovely lyric or a rare sunset, or a beautiful face? It is more important that you should feel the beauty of the parable than that you should understand it. In fact, perhaps the full understanding of it is not accessible to us.

Among the elements of beauty in the parable are economy of expression, not a word too many; and appeal to the imagination, giving us something to see with the mind's eye, or hear with the mind's ear. Thus emotions of awe and sublimity are awakened, as we envisage that house on the sand wrecked by the storm. There are simplicity and ease of understanding in the familiar part of the parable, and there are profundity and suggestiveness in its recondite meaning. There are harmony between the parts, proportion, and grace, the whole being a unity composed of related parts. There are appropriateness to the occasion and adaptation to the needs of men. The parable is a neat tool, whether it is revealing truth to friends or concealing truth from enemies. It has the beauty of truth—truth to nature and to human nature in its divine aspects. In short, like any work of art, the parable is the union of the real and the ideal, the material real with the spiritual ideal. And the union is so full and flawless that we call it beautiful.

Could you illustrate each of these elements in the beauty of a parable? Do you feel their truth? Once again read the following:

"Again the Kingdom of the Heavens is like a jewel merchant who is in quest of choice pearls. He finds one most costly pearl; he goes away; and though it costs all he has, he buys it" (Weymouth). Is it not a gem itself?

The parable may be regarded as the analogue of the miracle. This would mean that the parable and the miracle are both alike and unlike. Stop a minute and see whether you can find similarity as well as dissimilarity between the two.

How would it do to say that both the parable and the miracle show the supremacy of the spiritual, but the parable shows it in the region of thought, and the miracle in the region of action? In the one case Jesus was expressing his thought, in the other his power.

In this connection recall the unusual miracle of cursing the barren fig-tree—unusual because it is the only instance of Jesus' cursing an irresponsible thing. Can we suppose that this miracle was really intended as a parable, that is, as a condemnation of the unfruitful Pharisees? If so, in this instance, instead of speaking the word of the parable, Jesus performed the deed, to suggest spiritual truth. If this interpretation is acceptable, then this incident reveals the close connection of the parable and the miracle. In another connection we should study the use Jesus made of the miracle in his teaching; only a hint of it is given here.

The parables of Jesus suggest to us very interestingly something of his *philosophy of life*. By the phrase "philosophy of life" we mean one's general view of the world and its effect on conduct; or, we might convert the order of these terms and say we mean one's conduct and its effect on his general view of the world. Can you figure out what is coming? Try to do so.

Jésus saw analogies, comparisons, resemblances everywhere between the realm of matter and the realm of spirit. Thus there were two worlds, but they were related to each other. The first was a type or symbol of the second. It was less real than the other. It would pass away, but the other would not ("Heaven and earth shall pass away, but my words shall not pass away"). There is duality of materiality and spirituality, yet an analogical unity. Nature is a parable of Heaven, it means more than it says. The relations of man to his world symbolize the unseen relations of God to his children. This latter is the true and real world, existing now within the heart, and to abide forever. There is nothing here of the logical and intellectual interpretations of Plato, unless it be in his tales and myths (cf. The Tale of Er, at the end of the Republic), but rather the moral and the symbolic. Is it characteristic of the Greek genius to be intellectual and of the Hebrew genius to be pragmatic?

No doubt you have been wondering whether Jesus originated, or borrowed, or both borrowed and adapted the parable. Read the following:

"And the word of Jehovah came unto me, saying, Son of man, set thy face toward the south, and drop thy word toward the south, and prophesy against the forest of the field in the South; and say to the forest of the South, Hear the word of Jehovah: Thus saith the Lord Jehovah, Behold, I will kindle a fire in thee, and it shall devour every green tree in thee, and every dry tree:

the flaming flame shall not be quenched, and all faces from the south to the north shall be burnt thereby. And all flesh shall see that I Jehovah have kindled it; it shall not be quenched. Then said I, Ah Lord Jehovah! they say of me, Is he not a speaker of parables?" (Ezek. 20: 45-49.)

Ezekiel means that Jehovah will use the Babylonians to destroy utterly southern Judea and its capital Jerusalem, as explained plainly in the following chapter. There are many such parables in Ezekiel and in other Old Testament writers, as well as fables, riddles, allegories, proverbs, and the like. For beautiful parables, see II Sam. 12: 1-9, and 14: 1-13. Jesus knew three books—the Old Testament, the book of nature, and the book of life. He found parables in the Old Testament, and he originated parables of nature and of life to set forth the new message of the Kingdom of Heaven. Besides, everybody in the Orient tells stories. In sum, we may answer our question by saying that Jesus found, adopted, adapted, and perfected the parable.

This study of the parables could be considerably prolonged, for the subject is rich, and books have been written on it. But, for our purpose, we must conclude now with a few practical suggestions.

It is clear that the art of story-telling should be a part of the teacher's repertory. He should know what the four parts of a story are, should be able to discern these four parts in the parable, should exemplify them in the stories he writes or tells, and should know how to tell stories to a company.[2]

---

[2] On these points consult the author's "Story-Telling, Questioning, and Studying," N. Y., 1916.

In order to see how a story-teller retells the parables, see the volume by Dean Hodges, "When the King Came," pp. 166–175, and 240–267.

In a book of synonyms or in an unabridged dictionary, find out the difference between parable, allegory, simile, fiction, fable, illustration, and metaphor.

You should also determine your favorite parable as well as discover the favorite parables of the group.

And since the meaning of the parable is its essential part, you should state for yourself the meaning of each of the parables. For example, in the parable of the Tares, who sows the good seed? what is the field? what are the good seed? what are the tares? who sows these? what is the harvest? who are the reapers? what is the burning of the tares? what is the gathering of the wheat? Jesus himself answers all these questions in explaining the parable to the disciples (Matt. 13: 36–43).

Did Jesus intend all the parables to be interpreted in such detail? For example, should we try to say what the two pence are that the Good Samaritan gave to the inn-keeper?

In following up the study of the parables, the following references will be useful:

Articles in Hastings' "Dictionary of the Bible" and Hastings' "Dictionary of Christ and the Gospels."

Bruce, C. B., "The Parabolic Teaching of Christ," London, 1882.

Goebel, S., "The Parables of Jesus," Edinburgh, 1883.

Winterbotham, R., "The Kingdom of Heaven," 1898.

Any commentary on the gospels or any life of Christ.

Mabie, Hamilton Wright, "Parables of Life," 1903.

CHAPTER XII

HIS USE OF THE SCRIPTURES

Did Jesus know and use the Scriptures? What scriptures?

Did he know and use any scriptures not in our Old Testament?

How did the Jews entitle their scriptures?

What is the Apocrypha?

Why as a rabbi would Jesus use the Jewish scriptures?

How is your answer related to the principle of apperception?

Make a list of direct quotations from the Old Testament that Jesus used.

This can easily be done by using a New Testament with references, or the article on "Quotations" in Hastings' "Dictionary of the Bible," or "Dictionary of Christ and the Gospels."

Omitting duplicates, how many direct quotations do you find?

Why is it that some of the quotations do not seem to be exact? Look up "Septuagint."

Compare your list with the following:

1. "Man shall not live by bread alone, but by every word that proceedeth out of the mouth of God" (Matt. 4: 4; Deut. 8: 3).

2. "Thou shalt not make trial of the Lord thy God" (Matt. 4: 7; Deut. 6: 16).

3. "Thou shalt worship the Lord thy God and him only shalt thou serve" (Matt. 4: 10; Deut. 6: 13).

4. "Thou shalt not kill" (Matt. 5: 21; Exodus 20: 13; Deut. 5: 17).

5. "Thou shalt not commit adultery" (Matt. 5: 27; Exodus 20: 14; Deut. 5: 18).

6. "Whosoever shall put away his wife, let him give her a writing of divorcement" (Matt. 5: 31; Deut. 24: 1, 3).

7. "Thou shalt not forswear thyself" (Matt. 5: 33; Lev. 19: 12; Num. 30: 2; Deut. 23: 21).

8. "An eye for an eye and a tooth for a tooth" (Matt. 5: 38; Exodus 21: 24; Lev. 24: 20; Deut. 19: 21).

9. "Thou shalt love thy neighbor and hate thine enemy" (Matt. 5: 43; Lev. 19: 18).

10. "I desire mercy and not sacrifice" (Matt. 9: 13, 12: 7; Hos. 6: 6).

11. "Behold I send my messenger before thy face" (Matt. 11: 10; Mal. 3: 1).

12. "By hearing ye shall hear, and shall in no wise understand" (Matt. 13: 14, 15; Isa. 6: 9, 10).

13. "Honor thy father and thy mother" (Matt. 15: 4: Exodus 20: 12; Deut. 5: 16).

14. "He that speaketh evil of father or mother, let him die the death" (Matt. 15: 4; Exodus 21: 17; Lev. 20: 9).

15. "This people honoreth me with their lips," etc. (Matt. 15: 8, 9; Isa. 29: 13).

16. "He who made them from the beginning made them male and female" (Matt. 19: 4; Gen. 1: 27, 5: 2).

17. "For this cause shall a man leave his father and

mother, and shall cleave to his wife" (Matt. 19: 5; Gen. 2: 24).

18. "Thou shalt not kill, Thou shalt not commit adultery, Thou shalt not steal, Thou shalt not bear false witness, Honor thy father and thy mother; and, Thou shalt love thy neighbor as thyself" (Matt. 19: 18, 19; Exodus 20: 12–16; Deut. 5: 16–20).

19. "Out of the mouth of babes and sucklings thou hast perfected praise" (Matt. 21: 16; Psalm 8: 2).

20. "The stone which the builders rejected,

The same was made the head of the corner"

(Matt. 21: 42; Psalm 118: 22).

21. "My house shall be called a house of prayer: but ye make it a den of robbers" (Matt. 21: 13; Isa. 56: 7; Jer. 7: 11).

22. "I am the God of Abraham, and the God of Isaac, and the God of Jacob" (Matt. 22: 32; Exodus 3: 6).

23. "Thou shalt love the Lord thy God with all thy heart, and with all thy soul, and with all thy mind" (Matt. 22: 37; Deut. 6: 5).

24. "Thou shalt love thy neighbor as thyself" (Matt. 22: 39; Lev. 19: 18).

25. "The Lord said unto my Lord,

Sit thou on my right hand,

Till I put thine enemies underneath thy feet"

(Matt. 22: 44; Psalm 110: 1).

26. "I will smite the shepherd, and the sheep of the flock shall be scattered abroad" (Matt. 26: 31; Zech. 13: 7).

27. "Eli, Eli, lama, sabachthani" (Matt. 27: 46; Psalm 22: 1).

28. "And he was reckoned with transgressors" (Luke 22: 37; Isa. 53: 12).

29. . . . . "into thy hands I commend my spirit" (Luke 23: 46; Psalm 31: 5).

30. "The Spirit of the Lord is upon me," etc. (Luke 4: 18; Isa. 61: 1, 2).

31. "I said, ye are gods" (John 10: 34; Psalm 82: 6).

32. "He that eateth my bread lifted up his heel against me" (John 13: 18; Psalm 41: 9).

33. "They hated me without a cause" (John 15: 25; Psalm 35: 19; Psalm 69: 4).

This list is not complete.

What impression do you get as to the familiarity of Jesus with the letter of Scripture?

From what portions of the Scriptures does he quote most?

Upon what occasions in his life does he draw upon Scripture? For example, the Temptation? the first sermon in Nazareth? the Sermon on the Mount? in meeting criticism? in answering questions? in asking questions? in his relation to John? in his explanation of the use of parables? in cleansing the Temple? in announcing his death? in announcing the betrayal? in explaining opposition? on the cross?

How did he regard his own teaching, life, and death as related to Scripture? (See John 5: 39, 40.)

Is it likely that we have all the quotations he made from Scripture?

In answering a question like this, recall that scholars say that all the incidents reported in the gospels fall on only thirty-five different days throughout a period of some three years. See also the remarkable last verse in the gospel of John.

Also take this little problem in arithmetic. One third of the gospel of John is devoted to one week in the life of Christ. Suppose all his weeks during three years of public ministry had been equally full and equally fully reported, how many gospels the length of John's would have been necessary?

Did Jesus ever write out any of his teaching for preservation? Why not?

Upon what principle did some of his words survive?

How did he obtain this intimacy with Scripture? When?

What is his attitude toward Scripture in the Sermon on the Mount?

Did he accept it as final authority?

Continue this study by making a list of his references and allusions to the Old Testament without directly quoting it. This can be done by reading through one gospel with this thought in mind.

What will such a list show?

Compare your list with the following:

1. The Persecution of the Prophets, Matt. 5:12.

2. The Gift That Moses Commanded, Matt. 8:4.

3. Those Who Shall Sit Down with Abraham, and Isaac, and Jacob in the Kingdom of Heaven, Matt. 8:11.

4. Sodom and Gomorrah in the Judgment, Matt. 10:15.

5. "This is Elijah," Matt. 17:12; Matt. 11:14.

6. A Man's Foes (cf. Mic. 7:6), Matt. 10:36.

7. What David Did, Matt. 12:3.

8. How the Priests Profane the Sabbath, Matt. 12: 5.
9. Jonah and Nineveh, Matt. 12: 40, 41.
10. The Queen of the South, Matt. 12: 42.
11. The Blood of Abel, Matt. 23: 35.
12. The Days of Noah, Matt. 24: 37.
13. The Mourning of the Tribes of the Earth, Matt. 24:30.
14. The Sign of the Son of Man in Heaven, Matt. 24: 30.
15. Sitting at the Right Hand of Power, Matt. 26: 64.
16. The Widows in Israel, Luke 4: 25.
17. The Lepers in Israel, Luke 4: 27.
18. The Days of Lot, Luke 17: 28.
19. Lot's Wife, Luke 17: 32.
20. Searching the Scriptures, John 5: 39.
21. Moses "wrote of me," John 5: 46.
22. The Witness of Two Men, John 8: 17.
23. Ascending and Descending Angels, John 1: 51.
24. Lifting Up the Serpent, John 3: 14.
25. The Bondservant in the House, John 8: 35.
26. The Rejoicing of Abraham, John 8: 56.

You can easily identify these Old Testament allusions by using a reference Bible on the passages given. This list is not exhaustive.

You can also test your familiarity with the Old Testament by noting how many you need to look up.

How do you think your knowledge of the Old Testament compares with that which Jesus showed?

What do these allusions show as to the ability of Jesus to use the Old Testament? Was he bound by its letter? He evidently used its incidents freely and independently of the words reporting them.

Yet more. There are some references by Jesus to what

had been written that cannot be identified. Do you know of any?

Here is a partial list:

1. "The Son of man goeth, even as it is written of him." (Where?) Matt. 26:24.

2. "How then should the scriptures be fulfilled, that thus it must be?" (What Scriptures?) Matt. 26:54.

3. "But all this is come to pass, that the scriptures of the prophets might be fulfilled." (What prophets?) Matt. 26:56.

4. "Elijah is come, and they have also done unto him whatsoever they would, even as it is written of him." (Where?) Mark 9:13.

5. "Therefore also said the wisdom of God, I will send unto them prophets and apostles." (Where? What is "the wisdom of God"?) Luke 11:49.

6. "For these are days of vengeance, that all things which are written may be fulfilled." (What things?) Luke 21:22.

7. "He that believeth on me, as the scripture hath said, from within him shall flow rivers of living water." John 7:38. (Cf. Isa. 12:3 and Ezek. 47:1.)

8. "Not one of them perished, but the son of perdition; that the scripture might be fulfilled." (What Scripture?) John 17:12.

There are other passages of this kind. How do you explain them?

Was Jesus here referring to the general tenor and spirit of the Scriptures?

Is it conceivable that he may have referred to what was written in the mind of God?

Did Jesus tend to regard what had happened as the fulfilment of Scripture even when specific references are lacking?

Would such an attitude of mind make the endurance of suffering easier?

These questions rather reveal our ignorance than lead to knowledge.

However, what do such passages indicate as to the reliance of Jesus on Scripture? as to the way in which the thought of Scripture filled his mind?

There is such a thing as knowing Shakespeare or the Bible so well that one's literary or spoken style unconsciously reflects their form of expression. So Webster, Lincoln, and Ruskin knew the Bible.

Is it possible, similarly, that Jesus may have used Old Testament forms of expression naturally, without intending to quote?

In the light of this question study the following pairs of quotations:

1. "Blessed are they that mourn, for they shall be comforted." Matt. 5: 4.

"To comfort all that mourn." Isa. 61: 2.

2. "Blessed are the meek, for they shall inherit the earth." Matt. 5: 5.

"The meek shall inherit the earth." Psalm 37: 11.

3. "Blessed are the pure in heart, for they shall see God." Matt. 5: 8.

"He that hath clean hands and a pure heart." Psalm 24: 4.

4. "Neither by the heaven, for it is the throne of God; nor by the earth, for it is the footstool of his feet." Matt. 5: 34, 35.

"The heaven is my throne and the earth is my footstool." Isa. 66: 1.

5. "Seek, and ye shall find."   "If thou seek him, he will be
    Matt. 7: 7.   found of thee." I Chron. 28: 9.

There are some forty similarly parallel passages.

What conclusion do you draw?

We have seen quotations, and allusions, and similar literary form connecting the teaching of Jesus with the Scriptures.

A profounder line of inquiry would be to ask how his thinking is related to Old Testament thinking.

Are the matters that he makes fundamental also to be found in the Old Testament? God as father? (See Psalm 103: 13.) Love of God and neighbor? The Kingdom of God? (See Dan. 2: 44; 7: 27.)

With this thought in mind, compare the following passages:

"The sabbath was made for man, and not man for the sabbath." Mark 2: 27.

"Six days thou shalt do thy work, and on the seventh day thou shalt rest." Exodus 23: 12.

"Except one be born of water and the Spirit, he cannot enter into the kingdom of God." John 3: 5.

"I will sprinkle clean water upon you, and ye shall be clean . . . and a new spirit will I put within you." Ezek. 36: 25–27.

But is there any real Old Testament parallel for Matt. 5: 44: "Love your enemies"? Compare Job 31: 29, 30, Psalm 7: 4, and Exodus 23: 4.

Still another question. The Jews had religious writings which do not appear in our Old Testament, known as the Apocrypha. Was Jesus acquainted with these writings also?

Read the following passages and decide for yourself:
"Accustom not thy mouth to an oath;

And be not accustomed to the naming of the Holy
   One."

> Ecclesiasticus 23: 9.   (Cf. Matt. 5: 34, 35.)

"Reject not a suppliant in his affliction;

And turn not away thy face from a poor man.

Turn not away thine eye from one that asketh of thee,
And give none occasion to a man to curse thee."

> Ecclesiasticus 4: 4, 5.   (Cf. Matt. 5: 42.)

"Lend to thy neighbor in time of his need;

And pay thou thy neighbor again in due season."

> Ecclesiasticus 29: 2.   (Cf. Matt. 5: 42.)

"Forgive thy neighbor the hurt that he hath done
   thee;

And then thy sins shall be pardoned when thou
   prayest."

> Ecclesiasticus 28: 2.   (Cf. Matt. 6: 12, 14.)

The book of Ecclesiasticus or The Wisdom of Jesus the
Son of Sirach was probably written 100–50 B. C. It re-
sembles the Proverbs, is probably superior to Proverbs
in moral quality, and may be read with edification.

"But thou didst teach thy people by such works as
   these,

How that the righteous must be a lover of men."

> The Wisdom of Solomon, c. 100 B. C.

"And what thou thyself hatest, do to no man."

> Tobit 4: 15.   (Cf. Matt. 7: 12.)

Tobit, like Confucius, gives the Golden Rule in negative form.

What is your conclusion as to whether Jesus knew the Apocrypha?

Jesus does not quote directly from the Apocrypha in what has come down to us, but it is evident his thoughts are similar.

Should we then study the Apocrypha? (The Apocrypha was written in Greek and Latin. A revised version can be had from the Oxford University Press. It contains fourteen books. The original meaning of the term is "hidden." In the second century the meaning changed to "spurious." The titles of the fourteen books are: I and II Esdras, Tobit, Judith, The Remainder of Esther, The Wisdom of Solomon, Ecclesiasticus, Baruch, Song of the Three Holy Children, History of Susanna, Bel and the Dragon, Prayer of Manasses, and I and II Maccabees. These books are accepted as canonical, that is, "genuine and inspired," by the Roman Catholic Church, but are rejected by the Jews and the Protestant churches. Are writings or writers inspired? May inspiration be received from a writing not accepted as "inspired"?)

Let us turn briefly next to the question you have without doubt been raising all along, as we have been considering the relation of Jesus to the Scriptures existent in his day, namely, in what consists the *originality* of Jesus?

Original he was, else we should never have had a "New" Testament.

How do you answer the question?

In the following list of statements, check off the ones with which you agree.

Jesus was original in teaching the love of enemies.

He was original in selection and emphasis, that is, out

of a mass of Old Testament views he selected certain ones for primary emphasis.

He was original in clarifying, amplifying, and applying the views selected. (How many times is God referred to as "Father" in Old Testament, and in the New?)

He was original in substituting the spirit of love which fulfils law naturally for the law itself and its letter.

He was original and unique in living what he taught.

He was original and unique in his personal claim to fulfil Scripture, to be the Messiah. Jesus' becoming and being Christ is the new thing.

He is original in the universality of his vision, coupled with the individuality, not nationality, of his appeal.

He is original as is an artist who sits in the presence of the greatest of his predecessors, assimilating and absorbing until he comes into his own creative self-expression.

He is original and unique in being a racial man, that is, realizing the moral and religious capacities of the race— "the Son of Man."

He is original and unique in his unbroken sense of union and communion with God—"the Son of God."

With which statements are you not in agreement?

What statement of his originality would you add?

What other religion besides Christianity has ever bound up with its own sacred writings those of another religion? What is the significance of this fact?

Summarizing our study of how Jesus used Scripture, let me append certain statements of scholars. Check the ones with which you agree:

"The mind of Jesus was saturated with the Book of Isaiah."

"Jesus was an authoritative interpreter of the Old Testament."

"He had so absorbed the Old Testament that its ideals were his commonplaces of thought."

"Jesus joined the work which he did as closely as possible to that of the Old Testament prophets, using their authority for his teachings."

"Jesus was also a Prophet greater than any that had gone before him."

"The great ideas that were regulative of the Old Testament revelation were also those which guided the practice and conduct of our Lord" (cf. Matt. 3:15).

"The body of his teaching is everywhere permeated by Old Testament ideas and colored by Old Testament language."

"He subjected himself to its spiritual authority."

"Jesus recognized the process of evolution that took place in Old Testament revelation" (cf. his setting aside certain precepts of the law and his reference to Tyre and Sidon).

"Jesus used the Old Testament as the source of his own spiritual life."

"The Old Testament presents to our souls characters that are supremely worthy of our reverence because consciously centered in God and full of his power. It permits us to share the enthusiasm of the men who discovered the fundamentals of our religion and the character of our God. It is indispensable to complete discipleship of Christ, because it is the creator of the mould which his soul expanded."

"Higher values than these, religiously, there are not. No man save Jesus ever had the right to lay the book that offered these aside. And he made it immortal."[1]

---

[1] A. W. Vernon, "The Religious Value of the Old Testament," 1907, pp. 80, 81.

Why is the Old Testament "old"? Who made it so?

Is the New Testament still "new"? Will it ever become "old"?

Some final practicalities:

Jesus used the Old Testament for the growth of his own soul. Do we need it for the same?

He also used it as the common meeting-ground with the religious minds of his day. What analogous use should we make of it?

What should be the attitude of Christianity toward the Jewish religion today? of Christians toward Jews?

What should be the attitude of the missionary toward the religion and the religious writings of the people to whom he goes?

Can a Christian understand the mind of Christ without understanding Moses and Elijah, the law and the prophets? Recall the Transfiguration.

What does this study mean to you personally? That the moral and religious teacher should be a student of religious literature? Especially of religious literature of the highest inspirational value?

Such acquisition will enter into the fiber of his own personality, will affect the quality of his speech and conversation, and will so become the basis of his conscious and unconscious appeal to others. It would even be profitable to study the world's religious literature comparatively, and read some of the sacred writings of the Hindus, Persians, Chinese, and Arabs. In consequence biblical literature would mean not less but more.

Do we know enough?

What are we going to do about it?

CHAPTER XIII

HIS USE OF OCCASION

Leading educational thinkers are saying today that education must be vital, must grow out of a situation, must satisfy a felt need, must solve a real problem, nay, even must follow out a "project." A "project" is an assigned task in which the pupil is interested, which requires further study for its completion. In this way the ideas gained begin to "function" at once. All this means that education must be in immediate contact with actual living, and so not formal, not academic, not for its own sake.

Can you restate the viewpoint of the preceding paragraph in your own language?

Do you find yourself in agreement?

Would you say that Jesus assigned to the apostles a task in which they were interested, but which required further thought before its completion? What was that task?

Can you now foresee what is coming in our discussion of the use Jesus made of the natural occasion as it arose?

Do we really learn more in or out of school? Why?

Emerson said a boy learns more from the book under his desk than from the book on it. Do you agree? Why?

Have you noted who study more as a class, college or professional school students? Why is this?

What difference does it make in your study whether you have a purpose or not?

At this point recall one natural occasion arising in the

life of Jesus and the use he made of it to do or say something worth while.

Here follow some further illustrations of the same.

The Occasion	*Its Use*
Finding the traders in the Temple	Cleansing the Temple
Nicodemus came to him	Teaching the birth from above
There cometh a woman of Samaria	Transforming a life
The leper came to him	Cleansing physical life
The bringing of the palsied man	Spiritual and physical healing
He saw a man lying at the pool of Bethesda	Physical healing
The murmuring of the Pharisees at the disciples for plucking ears of corn on the Sabbath	Teaching the true relation of man and the Sabbath
"Seeing the multitudes"	The Sermon on the Mount
The coming of John's messengers	A message to John and a eulogy of John
Eating with Simon the Pharisee	Parable of the two debtors
The charge: "This man hath Beelzebub"	Teaching concerning the unpardonable sin
The coming of his mother and brethren	Teaching the supremacy of spiritual relationship
The disciples' question, "Why speakest thou unto them in parables?"	Teaching concerning the mysteries of the kingdom
The disciples request an explanation of the parable of the tares.	Teaching concerning the sons of evil
"Why eateth your master with publicans?"	Teaching concerning the whole and the sick

This list covers not over one fourth of the illustrations the gospels provide. Perhaps they are enough to illustrate adequately the point that it was characteristic of

Jesus to make use of the occasion as it arose. This is one of the reasons for the vitality of his teaching.

Make a supplementary list for yourself of the natural occasions Jesus used as they arose and the use he made of them either in action or speech. Doing this will bring home to you the meaning of the use of occasions.

Can you imagine Jesus letting an occasion slip?

Is it the custom for us to use the occasion or let it slip? Why do we do so?

What has the lack of courage and the lack of power to do with it?

What kind of a guest was Jesus, for example, in the home of Simon the Pharisee, or of Martha and Mary?

Was the personality of Jesus so dominating that he simply mastered every occasion, or do you think of him at times as merging his personality in that of the company, as, say, at the wedding in Cana?

Did Jesus ever make formal engagements in advance to appear at a certain place at a given time to heal, or teach, or preach?

Shall we conclude that the only kind of teaching Jesus did was occasional in character? If so, we must not neglect to add that he himself, being what he was, had much to do with causing these occasions to arise. Also, that he specifically made certain occasions, as when, having heard that the Pharisees had excommunicated the healed man born blind, Jesus sought him out and ministered to his soul (John 9: 35).

Can you think of other occasions that Jesus made?

Which is the greater opportunity for the minister, the Sunday sermon or the pastoral visit?

Which is the greater opportunity for the teacher, the lesson in manners and morals, or some good or bad act in school?

Do you agree with the judgment of Stanley Hall that Jesus "certainly was a master opportunist in seizing on every occasion, as it arose, to impart his precepts, and was in vital rapport with both the individuals and the groups he met"?

What difference would it make if we began now to be teachers of the occasional rather than the formal type?

CHAPTER XIV

HIS USE OF APPERCEPTION

In recently past time this term has been one to conjure with in educational theory. You might look up its story in an unabridged dictionary. Writers like Leibniz, Kant, Herbart, and Wundt use it in different senses. Its educational meaning is derived mainly from Herbart, and is easily grasped. It is this sense of the term that concerns us here.

By apperception we mean the interpretation of the new in terms of the old. The familiar or old ideas which we have in mind are what we must use in understanding the new. The old modifies the new, and the new enlarges the old. Thus a reciprocal process goes on between the old and the new, in which, however, the old is usually more influential in modifying the new than the new is in enlarging the old. In those rare cases in which the new displaces the old and itself becomes central in shaping still other incoming new impressions, we have a kind of mental conversion.

These statements are abstract and perhaps not fully intelligible. An illustration will help. A boy had seen and learned from his mother what a convict was, the kind that wears black and white striped clothing and works on the road. He had also learned what a mule was. With these ideas in mind they visit the zoo, and the boy sees what we know as a zebra. But he called it a "convict-mule." He was only interpreting the unknown in terms of the known. It is the best thing and the only thing we can do.

An old colored laundress remarked on seeing a parade of Red Cross nurses: "Befo' de Lawd, I nebber see so much white wash before in mah life!"

Roosevelt reported that as a boy he was afraid to go alone in a church building lest he should be eaten up by "the zeal of thine house."

A child hears sung the line of the old hymn: "The consecrated cross I'll bear" and understands it as referring to "the consecrated cross-eyed bear!"

So we know with what we have known. This is apperception.

Can you give other examples?

Now it is only common sense in teaching so to state one's views that they can easily connect up with what the class already has in mind. To fail to do so is not to be understood. To do so is to be both interesting and understood. The old Herbartian view was that the new should appeal to the old ideas, and this is still true, but the present view of Dewey, McMurry, and others is that the new should appeal to some present felt need or problem.

Can you think of any views stated by Jesus that involve the working of the same principle? Not, of course, that he thought in terms of modern psychology.

In this connection recall: "He that hath ears to hear, let him hear"; "To him that hath shall be given and he shall have abundance"; "Take heed how ye hear"; "Let him that readeth understand"; "Blessed are they that hunger and thirst after righteousness, for they shall be filled"; "Remember that every Scribe well trained for the Kingdom of the Heavens is like a householder who brings out of his storehouse new things and old" (Matt. 13: 52, Weymouth); "I came not to destroy, but to fulfil." So he seems to have recognized the working of the principle.

Can you recall instances of his use of apperception in his teaching?

Each one of the parables makes use of the more familiar to interpret the less familiar.

To the woman at the well he speaks of "living water."

To those seeking a sign he refers to the "signs of the times" which they could not discern, though they could read the weather signs.

When they told him his mother and brethren were standing without and would speak to him, he told them who his spiritual mother and brethren and sisters were.

In justifying his disciples in plucking ears of corn on the Sabbath, he put their critics in mind of what David did and of what the priests do on the Sabbath day as the basis for apperceiving what the disciples did.

He puts his synagogue hearers in Nazareth in mind of the Messianic prophecy of Isaiah as the basis for understanding himself (Luke 4: 16–30).

Succinctly he presents himself as "the bread of life," as "the light of the world."

Yet he was not received. John records that he came unto his own and his own received him not. He explains it by saying that darkness cannot understand light. "The light shineth in darkness, and the darkness apprehended it not" (John 1: 5). It was a case of failure to apperceive. The main reason was that to the Jews the expected

Messiah was a temporal deliverer, while Jesus taught that his kingdom was spiritual. In vain he tried to show them that the Messiah was David's lord, and so spiritual, and not necessarily his son, and so temporal. They could not see it so. Their mental eyes were blinded by their own prepossessions. Even the disciples after the resurrection were still earthbound enough to ask: "Lord, dost thou at this time restore the kingdom to Israel?" (Acts 1: 6.) So Jerusalem could not recognize the day of its visitation, the tragedy of which brought the tears from his eyes.

Perhaps Jesus' recognition of the absence of an apperceptive basis is clearest in his figurative portrayal of why his disciples, unlike John's, did not fast. The asceticism of John was not the standpoint from which to understand the festival character of the kingdom. "No one tears a piece from a new garment to mend an old one. If he did, he would not only spoil the new, but the patch from the new would not match the old. Nor does anybody pour new wine into old wine-skins. If he did, the new wine would burst the skins, the wine itself would be spilt, and the skins be destroyed. But new wine must be put into fresh wine-skins. Nor does any one after drinking old wine wish for new; for he says, 'The old is better'" (Luke 5: 36–39, Weymouth).

In this Jesus says plainly that the Baptist is not the apperceptive basis from which to understand the Kingdom.

Jesus desired and labored to be himself apperceived by his countrymen for what he took himself to be, but it could not be. His thoughts were not their thoughts. As

Stanley Hall writes: "The whole of life had to be reconstructed and brought under the light of new apperceptive centres in order to bring fitness to enter his Kingdom."

Only a few illustrations of his use of apperception were cited. Can you add others?

A useful, though prolix, work on this topic is Lange's "Apperception."

CHAPTER XV

HIS USE OF CONTRAST

What do you anticipate can be made of this topic?

Run down the following list of words with your eye and think the corresponding opposite in each case.

Good.

Light.

True.

Black.

Old.

Summer.

Positive.

Beautiful.

Health.

Spiritual.

God.

Did it require much time to do so?

Write the opposites in a parallel column.

Of course this is one form of association of ideas—that by contrast. You notice how natural and easy it is to have associations of this kind. Make a list of other pairs of opposites.

What are some of the effects of the use of contrast? Think of its use in art, in handling forms and colors.

Placing opposites over against each other reveals differences between members of a single group, exhibits the dissimilar qualities in the things compared, emphasizes their antagonism, has a pictorial quality and so appeals to the imagination, and is likewise an aid to attention and memory.

For all these reasons the use of contrast is a great aid in the art of expository teaching.

Did Jesus make use of the principle of contrast in his teaching? Make a list of illustrations involving contrast. Usually these illustrations are most obvious where the contrast is between just two persons, but often the contrast appears also in a more complex situation.

As used by Jesus the contrast is not introduced primarily for artistic purposes, but for didactic purposes. Still, its use so heightens the effect that artists readily spread such scenes on canvas, as, say, the two men in the temple, or the Last Judgment.

Let us study the following illustrations of contrast:

1. Lesson: The Fulfilling of the Law.

Formula of contrast: "Ye have heard that it hath been said unto you . . . but I say unto you."

These contrasts appear, of course, in the Sermon on the Mount.

How many times is the formula repeated? (See Matt. 5: 21, 22, 27, 28, 33, 34, 38, 39, 43, 44.)

2. Lesson: Sincerity in Religion.

Contrast: The hypocrites and Jesus' disciples.

These contrasts likewise appear in the Sermon on the Mount.

How many times is this contrast made? (See Matt. 6: 2-4, 5-15, 16-18.)

Study the use of the adversative "but" in the following passages: Matt. 5: 22, 28, 34, 39, 44; 6: 3, 6, 17. What is its effect?

3. Lesson: God the Common Father of All.

    Contrasts: The one lost sheep and the ninety and nine.
      The one lost coin and the nine.
      The one lost son and the elder brother.   (See Luke
      15.)
      What social classes are typified by each side of the
      contrast?

4. Lesson: True Obedience.

    Contrast: The two sons commanded to work in the
vineyard. Matt. 21: 23–32.

    Who are these two sons?

5. Lesson: True Treasure.

    Contrast: Treasure on earth and in heaven. Matt. 6:
19–21.

    What two classes are here intended?

6. Lesson: Watchfulness.

    Contrast: Wise and foolish virgins. Matt. 25: 1–13.

    What new feature of contrast appears in this illustration?

7. Lesson: The Final Separation of Good and Bad.

    Contrast: The sheep and the goats. Matt. 25: 30–40.

    How large are the contrasted groups in the illustration?

8. Lesson: The Real Neighbor.

    Contrast: The Priest, the Levite, and the Good Samaritan. Luke 10: 25–37.

    What variation in the use of contrast appears here?

    In the same way find the lesson taught and the contrast used in each of the following passages: Matt. 5: 17–20; Matt. 7: 24–27; John 4: 3, 14; John 4: 21, 22; Matt. 18: 21–25; Luke 12: 4, 5; Luke 12: 8, 9; Luke 12: 10; Luke 18: 9–14.

How is the principle of contrast as used in the parable of the Talents and the Pounds like, and also unlike, that in the parable of the Good Samaritan?

How does contrast appear in the parable of the Sower? in the parable of the Rich Man and Lazarus? in the directions concerning whom to invite to a supper?

Note that in the parable of the Prodigal Son the contrast is, as usual, between one and one; in the parable of the Good Samaritan between one and two; in the parables of the Talents and Pounds between two and one; in the parable of the Sower between one and three kinds of soil; in the parable of the Lost Coin between one and nine; in the parable of the Lost Sheep between one and ninety and nine; in the parable of the Virgins between five and five; and in the portrayal of the Last Judgment between two great groups embracing all. Have you still other variations to note?

Perhaps there is no phase of the method used by Jesus as a teacher that more clearly shows its esthetic quality than this of contrast. It reveals his feeling for the form of spoken discourse, as a part of one's effectiveness in presenting ideas.

If you were teaching the lesson of honesty to a group of boys and wanted to use the principle of contrast, how would you do it?

What is the danger in telling boys about dishonest boys?

CHAPTER XVI

HIS USE OF THE CONCRETE

The term "concrete" is associated by contrast with the term "abstract." What is not concrete is abstract, and what is concrete is not abstract. The table before you is concrete, but the quality of utility which it possesses in common with many other things is abstract.

It is easy to lay down a working line of distinction between the concrete and the abstract. What would you say it is? That which appeals to the senses is concrete, and that which does not appeal to the senses is abstract. Thus individual men are concrete, but the universal man is abstract. Yonder bluebird is concrete, but animal is abstract.

A difficulty arises regarding states of consciousness or some element of a state of consciousness. Is the sensation red, received from looking at a red object, abstract or concrete? The object is, of course, concrete. The sensation is open to inner observation, it appeals to the inner sense. As such it, too, is concrete. Any state of mind studied by introspection is concrete. So our principle holds—whatever appeals to the senses (outer or inner) is concrete.

Watch the following distinction carefully. We may have an idea of "animal" as a class in mind. In this case "animal" is the object of the idea. Now the idea in this case, being open to internal observation, is concrete, but "animal," the object of the idea, not being accessible to the senses, but only to thought, is abstract. Do you follow? If not, try again to get it.

Now, in the development of intelligence, which naturally comes first, the concrete or the abstract? The question means, Which naturally appeals more to children, sense reports or thought reports? A series of other questions will bring out the same idea. Which comes first, the particular or the general? the empirical or the rational? the percept or the concept?

Such being the case, let us ask whether we usually illustrate the concrete by the abstract or the abstract by the concrete. Do we use the visible to illustrate the invisible or the invisible to illustrate the visible? For your answer think of the concrete imagery like golden streets, palms, harps, crowns, with which our minds picture the abstract idea, heaven.

How important to the teacher of less mature minds than his own is the art of illustration? What does illustrating the abstract do for it? Does it make it more or less intelligible? vivid? clear?

A great philosopher, Kant, once wrote: "Concepts without percepts are empty, percepts without concepts are blind." Can you figure out what he meant? Why is it that a country boy may not be able to see the city for the houses? or a city boy the forest for the trees?

The Swiss educational reformer Pestalozzi affirmed that there must be a sense-basis for all instruction. What did he mean by it? Do you agree with him?

Now in what region, abstract or concrete, are principles? axioms? theorems? maxims? proverbs? commands? laws? life after death? all moral and religious truths? If these things are to be taught in a realizable way, how is it to be done?

So we come to our question: Did Jesus make use of the concrete in teaching the abstract? As a moral and religious teacher his field was the abstract. His audiences showed various degrees of unfitness and fitness to follow him. How did he bring abstract truth down to the level of their intelligence?

At this point make a list for yourself of all the illustrations of the concrete you can think of, or have time to find, in the teachings of Jesus.

Since the concrete is used to help convey the meaning of the abstract, make in a parallel column a corresponding list of the abstract lessons so taught. Do this for yourself first. In doing it you will find perhaps some difficulty in saying at times just what the abstract lesson is, and you may differ from others in interpreting the abstract meaning of the concrete illustrations. This helps to reveal the difficulty of understanding the abstract world. By the way, heaven may be concrete enough to those who are there, but to us now it is, as a place at least, conceived and not perceived, and so is abstract.

We could easily become philosophical at this point and ask whether the abstract ideas have objective existence or not, or whether they exist only as features of similarity in particular things, or even whether they are only class names. Does the concrete alone exist? Look up realism, conceptualism, nominalism, in the dictionary or some general history of philosophy.

We might also draw another line of distinction between

the concrete and the abstract, somewhat more philosophical, and say that the concrete is a whole, and the abstract is any part of that whole, as a tree is concrete and its leaf is abstract. On the first basis, as appealing to the senses, leaf would be concrete, too. This paragraph and the preceding will appeal to the abstract-minded.

The following will illustrate the use Jesus made of the concrete in teaching the abstract.

Concrete	Abstract
"Behold the birds"	Trust
"Consider the lilies"	"
'The wind bloweth"	The Spirit; Action
"This little child"	True Greatness
"This poor widow"	Genuine Benevolence
"Shew me a penny"	Civic Duty
"Who is my mother?"	Spiritual Kinship
"Seest thou this woman?"	True Hospitality
"Two sparrows"	Providence
"Hairs of your head"	"
Foxes	Homelessness
Grapes and figs	Fruitful Discipleship
"Fishers of men"	Personal Work
"What things ye have seen and heard"	Data for John's Judgment
Ox in the ditch	Humaneness
Sheep in the pit	"
Camel and needle's eye	Perils of Wealth
The cursed fig-tree	Penalty of Hypocrisy
Beam and splinter	Large and Small Faults
"The narrow way"	Difficulty of Being Good
"The strait gate"	" " " "
"Wolves in sheeps' clothing"	False Prophets
"Children of the bride-chamber"	Festal Character of the Kingdom
"Lift up your eyes to the harvest"	Vision of Human Need

"Serpents"	Wisdom
"Doves"	Harmlessness
"Cup of cold water"	Service
"Reed shaken in the wind"	One view of John
"Light of the world"	?
"Salt of the earth"	?
"The candle on the candlestick"	?
"My yoke"	?
"The face of the sky"	?
"The other cheek"	?

Each separate parable is a study in the concrete.

In addition every miracle was concrete, but to what extent were the miracles performed to teach abstract lessons? For what purpose were they primarily performed? To relieve suffering or distress or embarrassment? To prove his Messiahship?

Further, every event of his life was concrete and has been used by others to teach the abstract, though not so used in every case by himself. What events in his life were used by himself as concrete illustrations of abstract truths? Is this one: "If they have called the master of the house Beelzebub, how much more they of his household"?

Fill in for yourself the abstract meaning for the question marks in the second column above.

What additional examples have you of the concrete used to make plain the abstract?

What now may we as teachers of moral and religious truth learn from the use Jesus made of the concrete?

Suppose you had to teach the lesson of obedience, how would you do it? How did Jesus do it?

In teaching is it better to proceed from the concrete to

the abstract, or from the abstract to the concrete? Which did Jesus do in Matt. 6: 25–30? Is it from the abstract to the concrete back to the abstract again? How would this question be related to the intellectual attainment of the audience? Is it conceivable that before some audiences one might proceed from the abstract to the abstract? Would it be desirable?

Which is the bigger mistake, to talk to children in terms of the abstract without the concrete, or to talk to adults in terms of the concrete without the abstract?

In the preparation of the next lesson you have to teach, note its abstract and its concrete elements.

One big practical principle we derive from this study is this: *Never try to teach the abstract without attaching it to the concrete.* If you have to teach honesty to boys, tell true stories of boys who were honest when it was hard to be so, and so on.

Is that teaching principle just given abstract or concrete? How would you make it the other?

We have now repeatedly seen how entirely in accord with the best we know today in educational theory is the practice of Jesus. How do you account for this? Would you describe Jesus as "a born teacher"? Do you think he may have imitated any of his own teachers in the Nazareth synagogue school, or elsewhere? Do you suppose he just taught properly in a natural way? Do you think he may ever have considered the methods of teaching in a conscious way? With what problems may he have occupied his mind during "the eighteen silent years"? Of course, our answers here have to be held tentatively.

CHAPTER XVII

HIS USE OF SYMBOLS

The use of the symbol is very closely related to the use of the concrete. The symbol is itself something concrete set apart as a design or emblem to typify the abstract. Acts once performed as well as emblems repeatedly used may be symbolic. It is a very interesting subject, as we shall find.

Illustrations of symbols may be found in many departments of life besides religion. Write down a list of all the symbols that occur to you.

Just now a new set of symbols is developing in connection with aviation. For example, ═══════════, +++++++, ▮▮▮▮, are three symbols respectively for public roads, trolley tracks, and landing-stage.

Mathematics and chemistry have long had their symbols for addition, subtraction, multiplication, division, and the common elements and substances, like oxygen, hydrogen, hydrochloric acid, etc.

Is all language symbolic? How about abbreviations? the alphabet? the A. B. and other degrees? the letter on the college sweater?

Is paper money symbolic? Of what? How about the figures on coins?

Is the cipher printing of telegraphy symbolic? How about secret codes?

How are gems sometimes used as symbols? For example, emerald, moonstone, and opal for immortality, good luck, and bad luck.

There is a French school of poetry of symbolism, in which poetry is made to symbolize music in conveying emotions rather than ideas, of which Paul Verlaine is a leading exponent.

Astronomical and weather symbols abound.

There is even an insanity of symbolism in which the person treats events not as real, but as symbolizing some mystic meaning.

And of course we have symbolism in religion. Formal creeds are the best illustrations. Confessions, too, are symbols. The study of creeds and confessions is itself a special branch of theology known as "symbolics." Among familiar religious symbols are the cross, the dove, the ox, the lion, the eagle, for the second and third persons of the Trinity, Luke, Mark, and John. The swastika,卐, appears in many different forms, the meaning of which is doubtful. Many symbols of the sun are used in both religious and patriotic meanings, as on the Union Jack and the Japanese flags.

Why use symbols? They are a great economy, they appeal to the imagination, they suggest more than can be clearly stated, they are bonds of unity. Think of the signs of the deaf mute, of the Red Cross, of the Y M C A triangle, of the masonic badges, of fraternity pins, of church steeples, of the phallus and the lingam in some pagan worship, of insignia on banners and coins, and the like.

It is evident that symbols play a large rôle in religion and in life. There are some who hold that the gospel events themselves are primarily symbols of the common experiences in the life of humanity. Did you ever meet these views? For example, some regard the main events in the life of Jesus as symbolic of agriculture, saying that the first visit to Jerusalem typifies bringing the first fruits into the Temple, the baptism is the irrigation of the soil by rain, the temptation shows how grain cannot grow in some soil, the devil is unfruitfulness, the burial is the death of vegetation in winter, and the resurrection is the new life of springtime.

How does this impress you?

Is there a sense in which the main events in the life of Christ typify what should occur in the life of every Christian?

Did Jesus make use of symbols? Make a list of the possible symbols used by Jesus, and a parallel list of their meanings.

Compare it with the following list.

Symbol	*Meaning*
The Lord's Supper	Remembrance of Him
The Cross ("Let him take up his cross")	Sacrifice
Washing the disciples' feet	Humble service
Riding on an ass on Palm Sunday	Spiritual kingship
"Shake the dust off your feet"	Testimony against
The little child in the midst.	Humility and trust as qualifications for membership in the Kingdom.

Here are only six. Ought all these to appear in the list? Have any of these been regarded by some bodies of Christians as realities, not symbols? For example, footwashing and the Eucharist?

Can you think of any proper additions to the list? For example, can the cleansing of the Temple be regarded as a symbol of rejection of the sacrificial system?

It is not always easy to distinguish between a symbol and a concrete illustration. The symbol, however, is more or less set apart to render the specific service of recalling its associate. Thus the palm branch is a symbol of victory, and the anchor of hope. The concrete is any sensible thing. So all symbols are concrete, but not all concrete things are symbols. Thus, the ink bottle before me is concrete, yet not symbolic. However, an ink pot with a pen is an Egyptian hieroglyph signifying a scribe.

Some of the common symbols for Jesus himself are the Good Shepherd, the lamb, the lion, the fish, the Chrismon, and I.H.S. The reasons for symbolizing Jesus as the Good Shepherd and the lamb are obvio: . The Apocalypse describes Jesus as the lion of the tribe of Judah. The fish is an early Christian symbol of Jesus. The Greek word for fish is *ichthus*, the letters of which are the initials of five Greek words meaning Jesus Christ, Son of God, Saviour. The symbol was possibly chosen to throw the persecutors of Christianity off the track. The Chrismon is a monogram of the Greak *Chr.*, meaning *Christos*. I.H.S. is, of course, *Jesus hominum salvator*.

Notice that the remarkable thing about the symbols used by Jesus is that they are acts. Could the baptism of Jesus be regarded as symbolic?

Study Jeremiah 13: 1–14 and note the symbol of the girdle.

Why are such symbolic acts no longer performed?

Do you see any way to use symbolic acts today?

CHAPTER XVIII

HIS IMAGERY

From a recent book I quote the following:

"Dealing in likenesses, contrasts, and suggestions, figures flash word-pictures which vitalize all language, spoken or written, from conversation to poetry.

"The most forceful figures are consequently those based on imagery: simile, metaphor, synecdoche, metonymy, personification, apostrophe, and irony."[1]

This author discusses, in addition to these, allusion, allegory, parable, and hyperbole. This gives us a list of eleven figures of speech. If you are not already familiar with them, you can review them in any rhetoric, or even in an unabridged dictionary.

Now let us see what will happen if we inquire which of these figures Jesus used.

Simile. As the word, from the Latin, suggests, a simile says one thing is like another. "How often would I have gathered thy children together, even as a hen gathereth her chickens under her wings, and ye would not" (Matt. 23: 37).

Metaphor. The metaphor is an abbreviated simile, omitting the word of comparison. "Go and say to that fox" (Herod), Luke 13: 32.

Synecdoche. This figure puts a part for the whole, or a whole for the part: "I have meat [i. e. food] to eat that ye know not" (John 4: 32). This is also metaphor.

[1] E. R. Musgrove, "Composition and Literature," p. 142.

Metonymy. This figure names a thing by one of its attributes or accompaniments: "I must preach the good tidings of the kingdom of God to the other cities also" [i. e. to their inhabitants] (Luke 4: 43).

Personification. This figure endows things with personality: "The wind bloweth where it listeth" (John 3: 8).

Apostrophe. This figure addresses the absent as present: "Woe unto thee, Chorazin! woe unto thee, Bethsaida!" (Matt. 11: 21.)

Irony. In this figure one means the opposite of what the words say: "'Praiseworthy indeed!' he added, 'to set at nought God's commandment in order to observe your own traditions'" (Mark 7: 9, Weymouth).

Allusion. This figure is an indirect reference: "Destroy this temple and in three days I will raise it up" (John 2: 19).

Allegory. This figure is a sustained metaphor or simile: "I am the vine, ye are the branches" (John 15: 1–10).

Parable. A brief story with a moral or religious meaning: The Sower, The Good Samaritan.

Hyperbole, or rhetorical overstatement: "Ye blind guides, that strain out the gnat, and swallow the camel!" (Matt. 23: 24.)

Thus we have found in the recorded words of Jesus examples of every figure of speech mentioned by a modern author.

What impression do you gain from this fact?

Can you give additional illustrations of each of the figures so far discussed?

Let us turn to still other figures or forms of speech. I

am not so particular that you should be able to name these, as that you should feel their quality and sense the addition they make to spoken style.

"Follow me and I will make you fishers of men" (Matt. 4: 19).

"Let the dead bury their dead" (Matt. 8: 22).

"The last shall be first and the first last" (Matt. 20: 16).

"Whosoever would save his life shall lose it; and whosoever shall lose his life for my sake and the gospel's shall find it" (Mark 8: 35).

"It is easier for a camel to go through a needle's eye than for a rich man to enter into the kingdom of God" (Mark 10: 25).

"Ye know how to discern the signs of the heavens, but ye cannot discern the signs of the times" (Matt. 16: 3).

"Thou art Peter [a stone] and upon this rock I will build my church; and the gates of hell shall not prevail against it" (Matt. 16: 18). What is the meaning of this?

"They that have authority over them [the Gentiles] are called Benefactors" (Luke 22: 25).

"If a house be divided against itself that house cannot stand" (Mark 4: 25).

"Thou hearest with one ear, but the other thou hast closed" (reputed saying).

"Can the blind lead the blind?" (Luke 6: 39).

"The rich man also died and was buried" (Luke 16: 22).

"Neither do men light a lamp and put it under the bushel" (Matt. 5: 15).

On this passage one writer[2] remarks: "The saying of

2Alex. A. Duncan, Art. "Bushel," in "Dictionary of Christ and the Gospels."

our Lord is as picturesque as it is forcible. It gives us a glimpse into a Galilean home, where the commonest articles of furniture would be the lamp, the lampstand, the *seah* measure, and the couch. And who could fail to apprehend the force of the metaphor?"

"Cast out first the beam out of thine own eye" (Matt. 7: 5).

"Give not that which is holy unto the dogs" (Matt. 7: 6).

"Do men gather grapes of thorns?" (Matt. 7: 16.)

"If he shall ask an egg, will he give him a scorpion?" (Luke 11: 12.)

"Ye serpents, ye offspring of vipers, how shall ye escape the judgment of hell?" (Matt. 23: 33.)

"They that are whole have no need of a physician" (Mark 2: 17).

"Many good works have I showed you from the Father; for which of those works do ye stone me?" (John 10: 32.)

"The Pharisee stood and prayed thus with himself" (Luke 18: 11).

"It is not meet to take the children's bread and cast it to the dogs" (Mark 7: 27).

"If I by Beelzebub cast out demons, by whom do your sons cast them out?" (Luke 11: 19.)

"Sound not a trumpet before thee" (Matt. 6: 2).

"Ye are like unto whited sepulchres" (Matt. 23: 27).

"Ye build the sepulchres of the prophets and garnish the tombs of the righteous" (Matt. 23: 29).

What are some other striking passages you would add to this list?

Name as many of the figures of speech as you can.

Is there satire? sarcasm? wit? raillery? irony? the grotesque? humor? play on words? paradox?

An unabridged dictionary or a book of synonyms will tell you the difference between some of these terms.

Historically, is language more forceful before or after grammarians have analyzed it? Of course it would take a psychological student of the history of literature to answer this question definitely. The suggestion contained in this question is that the language of Jesus is more forceful because he had studied the three books of Scripture, nature, and man, and not the science of language. Some one has said that the critic is the man who can't.

Not to confine your attention to striking isolated passages, read the discourse of Jesus on "The End of the World" in Matt. 24 and 25, noting the wonderful imagery.

Imagery is the poetic element in prose. It adds a light and sparkling quality. This effect is due to emotion combined with imagination. It increases the pleasure of both listening and reading.

Really great teachers, especially teachers of ultimate things, must have a poetic cast of mind, to suggest to learners more than can be told about truth. Such a teacher's mind can play with truth, it is not in bondage to literal facts. Could you name half a dozen such world teachers?

But imagery easily leads to misunderstanding, if it is read as prose by prosaic minds. Jesus was not only a master of imagery, he also sensed the danger of its being misunderstood, and warned against it: "The words that I have spoken unto you are spirit, and are life" (John 6:

63). "The letter killeth, the spirit maketh alive" (II Cor. 3: 6). Imagery means not what it says, but what it means to say. The observance of this principle of exegesis would prevent many a dispute.

The New Testament rewritten without imagery would be less subject to misunderstanding, but it would be stale and flat, even if such a rewriting were possible. Try to state the meaning without imagery of "Ye are the salt of the earth . . . ye are the light of the world." Such an effort reveals how Jesus saved words, packed words with meaning, feathered them with imagery, and set them flying on the winds of the world. He taught with emphatic seriousness: "And I say unto you, that every idle word that men shall speak, they shall give account thereof in the day of judgment" (Matt. 12: 36).

What does a study of the imagery of Jesus mean for us practically? What effect has it on our reading of the New Testament? If we could use imagery, how would it affect our utterance in teaching?

CHAPTER XIX

CROWDS OR INDIVIDUALS?

Did Jesus as a moral and religious teacher make his appeals primarily to crowds or to individuals?

What is your first impression? Think it over carefully and note whether your first impression is confirmed.

Which is the customary view—that Jesus worked mainly with crowds or with individuals?

Is the question itself valuable enough to consider? It has some bearing on the method of any Christian worker —should he endeavor mainly to reach crowds or individuals?

Does a great evangelist appeal primarily to crowds or to individuals? Was the work of Jesus of this type?

Is the so-called "mass-movement" in India today primarily crowd action or individual?

Should today's program of the Church follow the method of Jesus?

Give some answer, however tentative, to these questions now. Our study may change some of these answers.

What are some of the crowd occasions in the life of Jesus?

Repeatedly he taught in the synagogues on the sabbath day, especially in Galilee, including Capernaum and Nazareth. Many of his cures were wrought on these occasions, some of which we will note presently.

Is it not significant that when his home city rejected

him, he should choose as a center of operations a larger and more centrally located city—Capernaum? "So he came down to Capharnahum, a town in Galilee, where He frequently taught the people on the Sabbath days" (Weymouth, Luke 4: 31. Cf. Matt. 4: 13–17).

During the second year of his public ministry, "the year of popularity," he was constantly accompanied by crowds, from Capernaum, from other parts of Galilee, from Decapolis (the Ten Towns), from Jerusalem and Judea, from beyond Jordan, from Idumea in the extreme south, and from Tyre and Sidon in the west. Just how large these "multitudes" were we cannot say, but the feeding of the four thousand, and the five thousand "beside women and children," may give us some idea. There was a period when the new teacher gave every appearance of being backed by a popular movement. These crowds, it is true, for the most part did not really understand that his call involved sacrifice. They came to be healed, to see works of healing, to see the new rabbi, to hear his wonderful words, and even to eat of the loaves and fishes. Rumors and reports helped to bring them, in response to many-tongued social suggestion.

Jesus seems to have directed his work mainly toward the cities and villages (Luke 8: 1–3). "I must go also into the next towns," he would say. He worked by design in the centers of population, though not exclusively there. He would send messengers ahead to prepare the village for his coming. He saw cities, as he saw multitudes, as he saw women, as he saw children, as, too, he saw individuals. Some of these cities later he rebuked because they repented not, though mighty works had been done in them—Bethsaida, Chorazin, Capernaum.

At times Jesus suffered inconvenience because of the crowds. They thronged him, they kept him so busy that at times he and the disciples had not enough leisure to eat, they kept his mother and his brethren from getting at him, they followed him when he would try to leave them behind, they awaited his coming on the other side of the lake, they continued with him for days, they would even come to take him to make him a king.

Was Jesus the master as well as the ministering servant of crowds? He had compassion on them as sheep scattered without a shepherd. He would have them sit down by companies and would feed them. He would send them away himself, after first telling his disciples where to go. By what method did he bid them depart? He would leave them behind unawares, and go up in the mountain to pray, or take his disciples away into a desert place and rest awhile. He would get in a boat and speak to them gathered on the lake-side. He would heal their sick, as many as came. He would speak to them the beatitudes and other wonderful words of life.

A multitude was present when he healed the paralytic in the synagogue in Capernaum, and the man with the withered hand, and the servant of the centurion, and the dumb demoniac. Can you find other instances of healing when a multitude was present?

A great multitude went with him to Nain when the widow's son was raised, and to the home of Jairus when his daughter was raised, and to the home of Martha and Mary when Lazarus was raised.

Jesus attended the annual religious festivals (passover, dedication, tabernacles) of the Jews in Jerusalem where there were always crowds. Once or twice he cleansed the Temple at such a time, as well as taught and healed.

He freely attended festive social gatherings, as the wedding at Cana, or the great feast made for him in Capernaum by Matthew Levi, one of his chosen disciples, or the dinner in the home of Simon the Pharisee in Bethany. And something always happened when he was guest. Or was it the case that no record was made of the social occasions he graced when nothing happened? Can you find other such occasions of a social nature?

To the multitude he praised the faith of the Roman centurion, eulogized John the Baptist, spoke the parables as a mode of selection from the crowd, addressed the Sermon on the Mount, told them to believe on him whom God had sent, uttered the allegory on "the bread of life," justified healing on the sabbath, extended the invitation at the feast of the tabernacles to come unto him and drink, and warned them against the leaven of the Pharisees, which is hypocrisy. What else did he say upon different occasions to the multitudes? Note particularly Luke 14: 25–35.

In what esteem did the social mind of the multitudes hold Jesus? It was very different at different times. They were amazed at his works, they heard his words gladly because of their note of authority, they held that a great prophet had arisen among them, that God had visited his people, that he had done all things well, that it was never so seen in Israel, that the Messiah himself could not do more wonderful signs, that he was John the

Baptist, or Elijah, or Jeremiah, or one of the old prophets, or the Son of David, that he was a Samaritan and had a devil, that he was beside himself, that he should be crucified.

Can you find still other expressions of the popular mind concerning him?

What do you think as to whether Jesus preferred to appeal to crowds or individuals?

Let us see some of the individuals to whom he ministered. Recall as many as you can. They include each of the Twelve, Nicodemus, the woman of Samaria, the son of the nobleman at Capernaum, the man with the spirit of an unclean devil, Peter's wife's mother, the leper, the paralytic, the thirty-eight-year invalid at Bethesda's pool, the man with the withered hand, the servant of the centurion in Capernaum, the son of the widow of Nain, the sinful woman who anointed him, Simon the Pharisee, Mary Magdalene, Joanna, Susanna, the dumb demoniac, the woman of the multitude who blessed the womb that bore him, the two Gadarene demoniacs, the daughter of Jairus, the two blind men, the daughter of the Syrophœnician, the deaf stammerer, the blind man of Bethsaida, the demoniac boy, the woman taken in adultery, the seventy sent on a mission two by two, the questioning lawyers (two), the Pharisee who dined him, one of the lawyers who felt that Jesus cast a reproach on his class, one of the multitude who wanted Jesus to divide an inheritance for him, the bowed woman, Herod, the man with the dropsy, the ten lepers, the rich young ruler, Martha, Mary, Lazarus, one born blind, the mother of James and John, the two blind men at Jericho, one of whom was Bartimæus, Zaccheus, Caiaphas, Pilate, the thief on the cross, and his mother.

Are some omitted? How many are here?

What had Jesus done for these individuals?

How many of these individuals had Jesus served in the presence of a crowd? How many privately?

Why did he sometimes take the afflicted individual out of the city or crowd in order to effect a cure?

Was any group cure effected? (Would that of the ten lepers be such?)

Is it fair to say that in some way personal relations had been established with each of the seventy who were sent forth two by two?

What shall we now say as to whether Jesus dealt by preference with crowds or individuals?

Can we be sure of our answer?

Does the "Great Commission" put the emphasis on the crowd or the individual?

Which was more abiding, his work with crowds or with individuals?

Does the resurrected Christ of the record still minister to crowds or only to the disciples?

In the teaching concerning the mote and beam in the eye, some think Jesus underestimated the value of public judgment and social criticism. What do you think?

Doubtless for some persons it is better to work with crowds, for others it is better to work with individuals. Recall Billy Sunday and Miss Margaret Slattery. Can you distinguish the type of person who should work with crowds from the type that should work with individuals?

With whom was his most careful work done, crowds or

individuals, if we can distinguish degrees of carefulness in his work?

Of course, it is true that often he reached crowds by means of individuals, when any act of healing or word of teaching was done for an individual in the presence of a crowd.

And it is, of course, also true that often he reached individuals by means of the crowds to whom he spoke. Some who came to scoff remained to pray. Others who came to take him went away charmed by his matchless words.

A personal conclusion: Jesus began with individuals, continued with crowds, and ended with individuals, during the three successive main periods of his ministry. He worked by preference and most successfully with individuals, because of the very nature of crowds. In fact, he did not trust crowds, nor himself to them, as he trusted individuals.

References:

Taylor, R. B., Art. "Crowd" in "Dictionary of Christ and the Gospels."

Dundas, W. H., Art. "Multitude," "Dictionary of Christ and the Gospels."

Omun, John, Arts. "Individual," "Individualism," and "Individuality" in same Dictionary.

Le Bon, G., "The Crowd."

Baldwin, J. M., "The Individual and Society."

Fite, Warner, "Individualism."

CHAPTER XX

EDUCATION BY PERSONAL ASSOCIATION

What does this title suggest to you?

It is a pedagogical truism that we teach more by what we are than by what we say. Such is the influence of personality. We learn by association with persons. All that goes by the name of suggestion and imitation is at work when one person is thrown in contact with another.

The great moral and religious teachers of the race have associated with themselves a group of intimate learners, or disciples, that they might learn not so much the lessons as the way of their teacher, and that so by personal witnesses the blessed truth might be passed on to others and so on to others. So did Confucius, so did Buddha, so did John the Baptist, and so did Jesus. Some of his disciples in turn likewise had associates, as Mark with Peter. Paul, too, had associates in his work—Silas, Barnabas, and others (cf. Acts 13: 13).

Jesus attached these learners to himself by "calling" them, once, twice, or even perhaps three times, under different circumstances. Andrew and John had first been disciples of the Baptist, who directed their attention to Jesus as he walked. Then they were called once or twice by the lakeside. The words of the call were few, simple, direct, personal: "Follow me." In the first intent it was a call to personal association and then to all that might flow from it.

Mark 3: 14 makes it plain that the purpose of the call was that they might first be "with him" and then that he

143

might "send them." Thus the main secret of the training of the twelve was association and its main objective was service.

These twelve chosen ones, perhaps twelve because of the tribes of Israel, were Galilean fishermen, and tax-gatherers, and others. Only Judas was from Judea. They were all innocent of the learning of the rabbinical schools of the time—their occupations show this—but not of the religious customs of the Jews, which were theirs also. Doubtless Jesus regarded them as fresh wine-skins, fit receptacles of his own new wine of religious truth. They were not always apt pupils, but their hearts were loyal, except that of Judas at the end, and though the crucifixion was a rude jolt to all their hopes, the resurrection restored their confidence in their Leader. So in the end that which they had seen and heard through personal association—"the grace and truth that came through Jesus Christ"—was triumphant in their lives. Someone has defined Christianity as "the contagion of a divine personality."

There seem to have been several concentric circles of persons about Jesus. In the innermost circle came Peter, James, and John, of whom John seems to have been nearest the heart of Jesus. Then came the others of the twelve. Then perhaps the seventy apostles. Then perhaps the company of the ministering women (Luke 8: 2, 3). Then the multitudes. Finally the hostile critics. The line of division was the degree of spiritual insight. To each and all Jesus gave himself according to their receptive ability. To all the parables are spoken, to the chosen few the mysteries are explained.

Would you say that Jesus individualized his learners? Think carefully of this question. Some of the disciples of Jesus appear to us now as such vague personalities. What do we know of Bartholomew, and James the son of Alphæus? What finally became of the seventy who had been sent forth?

Some students of the temperaments of the early followers of Jesus have concluded that Peter was nervous, John was sanguine, Philip was phlegmatic, and that each of the disciples not only had a distinct temperament, but was chosen on this account by Jesus, who in doing so revealed his power to recognize and control all types of men. How do these views impress you? Some regard St. Paul as choleric.

To make our study of the individualizing of the disciples by Jesus concrete, let us consider the most obvious case, that of his treatment of Peter.

Recall the characteristics of Peter and the way of training him used by Jesus.

The records represent Peter as having what William James calls "the precipitate will," that is, he was impulsive, rash, impetuous, bold, of the motor type. Perhaps his foil in all these respects was Thomas. Peter's name usually heads the list of the disciples, though he was not the first called. His leadership seemed natural. He was the regular spokesman for the group, not that he had been so delegated. It was Peter who answered for all the decisive question: "Whom say ye that I am?" On the mount of transfiguration he wanted to build material tabernacles for spiritual beings. He alone would prove that the appearance on the water was Jesus by walking out to him. He it was who began to rebuke Jesus for proposing to submit to suffering. He alone of the disciples protested against his feet being washed by Jesus. Most stoutly of all he affirmed he would not deny Jesus. He rashly drew his sword and uselessly cut off the ear of the servant of the high priest in the Garden. Though John outran him to the tomb, Peter was the first to enter. He cast aside his garment and swam ashore to meet his recognized and resurrected Lord. These are some of the things that show the kind of man Peter was.

How did Jesus develop Peter?

He called him to a difficult task—to catch men alive. Such tasks help to tame impetuous natures.

He gave him a new name—in the Hebrew Cephas, in the Greek Peter—signifying what he wanted him to become.

He visited him in his Capernaum home and healed a sick member of his family.

He placed heavy responsibility upon him, giving him "the keys," making him the group leader.

He allowed him to do an adventurous thing and fail—trying to walk on the water. Not that Peter, being a fisherman and a swimmer, should have felt a panic of fear at beginning to sink.

He rebuked him: "Get thee behind me, Satan," a rather humiliating address to one who had just been made the keeper of the keys.

He corrected his reliance on physical force: "Put up the sword into the sheath."

He warned him concerning the denial: "Before the cock crow twice, thou shalt deny me thrice." Was this really a warning or a statement of a predestined fact?

After the denial Jesus forgave Peter and re-commissioned him. The resurrection angel mentioned Peter especially by name: "Go tell his disciples, and Peter." The repeated commission given Peter: "Feed my sheep," "feed my sheep," "feed my lambs," bound Peter again in personal loyalty to his Lord.

Did this training make Peter rock-like? The tradition is that on suffering crucifixion under persecution, Peter requested that it might be with head down, that he die not as his Lord.

Can you similarly suggest the characters of James and John, and how Jesus trained them? For example, what is "Boanerges"? Did John begin by being an apostle of love, as he ended?

Can you mention some of the features of the group training that the twelve received? For example, in caring for the physical body? in encouragement? in prayer? in love? Consult Mark 6: 31, 5: 36; Luke 22: 32; John 13: 1.

What is the significance of the fact that Jesus would address the disciples at times as "children," "lads," "little flock"? (See Mark 2: 5, 10: 24; Luke 12: 32; John 13: 33, 21: 5.)

What are some differences between a teacher today before his class and Jesus with the twelve?

The twelve were dependent on Jesus for their training. Was he also in a measure dependent on them for companionship and strength? See Luke 22: 28, and remember the agony in the garden.

Name some respects in which Christianity in its history has exemplified this same reliance on the principle of human association.

It is sometimes said that the Church is in the New Testament, but not the Y M C A. Is the principle of the Y M C A there?

What further additions would you make to this discussion?

CHAPTER XXI

MOTIVATION

By the "motive" of an act we mean what? You are now doing something. Why? You have in the past undertaken some accomplishment. Why did you do so? Perhaps you are now in the midst of some undertaking, as a student in a school. Why?

We mean two things by "motive," either the antecedent reason or the consequent purpose of an act. So the motive is what *moves* us. We are moved both by an impulse behind the act and by the thought of a result to be accomplished. Thus, a man responds to the dinner call. The antecedent reason may be the sensation of hunger, or the fear that unless he goes he may be late and miss his meal altogether. The consequent purpose is that he may eat and be satisfied and nourished for his work. This is "consequent" because it follows the act, though the purpose itself that this result be accomplished is antecedent to the act.

May there be action without purpose or end? Certainly, all instinctive and involuntary action is of this type. A man sits on a tack and rises reflexly. There was an antecedent reason, but no consequent purpose, nor time to formulate one, though of course there is a desirable result.

May the two meanings of "motive" be reduced to one? Perhaps so, in this way: Anything which moves us to act or tends so to do is a motive. But even so, we have to distinguish between sensations and feelings as impelling us to action and intellectually presented ends voluntarily chosen to be accomplished. In sum, then, a motive is any ground for our action, either a felt antecedent of the act or an anticipated and chosen consequent of the act.

You will not mind first mastering this little bit of antecedent psychology in view of the consequent use we will make of it.

Now, how are teachers concerned with all this? What would you say? Simply this: We get no action from pupils without first awakening motives. And some motives are more effective and some more desirable than others. To avoid physical pain is a very effective motive —is it the most desirable motive?

What are some effective motives?

What are some desirable motives?

What is the problem of the teacher in motivation? It might be stated in this way: To make the desirable motives effective.

Among effective motives are the avoidance of pain, the securing of pleasure. Among desirable motives are doing right for right's sake, securing the common welfare, and the like. In certain instances, the effective motive may be desirable, as securing relief from toothache. In the case of properly trained people, the desirable motives are also effective, as when for the common good one subordinates his own interest.

The various motives which move men to action number so many that, if possible, it would be well to group them. Could you suggest any way of classifying the motives?

We might say that some acts are exclusively for self,

some mainly for self and partly for others, some partly for self and mainly for others, and some exclusively for others.

Would you allow that these four classes exist?

If so, we have the following four groups of motives: (1) egoistic, (2) *egoistic*-altruistic, (3) egoistic-*altruistic*, and (4) altruistic. As a matter of fact, some deny the existence of the first and fourth groups.

For the average person, which groups of motives are most effective?

For the properly trained person?

Which groups of motives are most desirable?

It may seem that we are a long time in coming to the question, which is, To what motives did Jesus appeal?

Make a list of these motives.

Classify them according to the four groups given above.

What are your results?

In each of the following passages, determine first to what motive Jesus is appealing and second, how this motive should be classified.

The Wise and Foolish Man, Matt. 7: 24–27.

Results of Belief and Unbelief, John 3: 16.

The Sheep and the Goats at the Judgment, Matt. 25: 31–46.

Seeking the Kingdom of God First, Matt. 6: 33.

"What then shall we have?" Mark 10: 28–31.

True Greatness, Matt. 20: 21–28.

Cross-Bearing, Matt. 16: 24–27.

The Call of Nathanael, John 1: 47–51.

The Conversation with the Samaritan Woman, John 4: 4–38.

"Fishers of Men," Mark 1: 16–18.
Idle Words, Matt. 12: 36, 37.
The Unpardonable Sin, Mark 3: 28, 29.

What are your conclusions?
To which group of motives did Jesus mainly appeal?
How high did he set the standard of motive?
How effective were these motives at the time?
How effective have they since proved themselves to be?
Is it hard or easy to be a Christian?
Why in the course of nineteen centuries has the world
not become Christian?
Would you regard the idealism of Jesus as practical?

In speaking of the motives in men to which Jesus appealed, we should distinguish between the motives he intended to arouse, and those naturally aroused without its being intended. Thus, some followed him because they ate of the loaves and were filled, for which they received his rebuke. His intention in feeding them was to relieve their distress, not to secure a following. See John 6: 25–27. In the same connection, in removing the lower motive he appealed to a higher motive: "Work not for the food which perisheth, but for the food which abideth unto eternal life."

We may distinguish not only the egoistic from the altruistic motives, but also the natural or intrinsic from the artificial or extrinsic motives or incentives. Can you draw this distinction in advance?

If a pupil works at his algebra because he has to, or because he is promised some reward by his parents if he does well in it, then his motive is artificial or extrinsic.

If, however, he is interested in it and wants to do it, his motive is natural or intrinsic.

Thus an intrinsic motive is one growing out of the work itself or its natural consequences, while an extrinsic motive is one growing out of some external or arbitrary addition to the thing being done.

Is studying a lesson in order to avoid a penalty an intrinsic or extrinsic motive? Is studying a subject not because one is interested in it but because it is required for admission to college an intrinsic or extrinsic motive? What kind of motive is it if one studies for the sake of the personal development that comes from study?

Review the motives to which Jesus appealed. Are they intrinsic or extrinsic? Are they both? See particularly Mark 10: 28-31, and Mark 9: 43-49.

When are we justified in using extrinsic motives? When not justified? What have maturity and training to do with this matter?

In this connection recall the teaching of Jesus: "A disciple [or learner] is not above his teacher, nor a servant above his lord. It is enough for the disciple that he be as his teacher, and the servant as his lord" (Matt. 10: 24, 25).

By what motives was Jesus himself animated?

Make a list of these motives.

How would you classify them? See Mark 1: 38, Luke 4: 43, John 15: 13, Heb. 12: 2, and many other passages.

Would you say that the motives of Jesus were in the third or the fourth class?

To draw our conclusions, to what group of motives in men did Jesus mainly appeal? By which group was he himself mainly moved? Is it possible to act from exclusively altruistic motives?

What may we learn from this study? Shall we appeal to the altruistic and intrinsic motives when they will be effective; otherwise, to the egoistic and extrinsic?

In answer to some of these last questions the author has only impressions which he prefers not to state until they can be corrected or confirmed by the findings of a group judgment.

CHAPTER XXII

DID JESUS APPEAL TO THE NATIVE REACTIONS?

This question .neans, did Jesus stimulate the instincts and innate tendencies of man? If so, he touched the primordial springs of all action, he sounded the depths of human nature. If not, his appeal does not reach down to the oldest elements in the human frame.

The question is important, for it helps us to understand whether Jesus released all the energies of human nature, and in what sense, and so we may see whether and to what extent his teachings meet the profoundest needs and demands of human nature.

What are these native reactions? According to James,[1] they are:

Fear; Love; Curiosity [or "Wonder"]; Imitation; Emulation; Ambition; Pugnacity; Pride (these four are called "the ambitious impulses"); Ownership; Constructiveness.

According to MacDougall,[2] the instincts and innate tendencies are: Fear; Disgust; Curiosity; Pugnacity; Self-Assertion ("Pride"); Self-Abasement; Parental ("Love"); Sex; Gregariousness; Acquisition ("Ownership"); Construction; Sympathy; Suggestion; Imitation; Play; Rivalry ("Emulation"); Habit; Temperament.

In MacDougall's list, based on very careful analysis, the

[1] "Talks to Teachers," Chap. VII, N. Y., 1899.
[2] "Social Psychology," Chaps. III and IV, Boston, 1918.

innate tendencies, which are non-specific in character in contrast with the specific instincts, begin with sympathy.

Whether Jesus himself evinced all the instincts of man we cannot now consider, having treated this question elsewhere.[3] And it would take us too far afield now to treat exhaustively the present question, and show from the gospels all the appeals to each of the native reactions of man.

It will be noted that MacDougall's list includes all of James's, unless it be ambition, which is very complex and involves considerable ideation.

At this point, go carefully through MacDougall's list and check every entry to which upon reflection you think Jesus did appeal. Are there any omissions? If so, which? Are you fairly sure about the entries checked? If you are not quite clear what is meant by any entry, look it up in James or MacDougall. Of course, it is a new question, this reading of the teachings of Jesus in terms of biology, and one probably very far from his own consciousness, but it is one in which our day is very much interested. Yet there can be but little objection to raising such a question, for one good way to test how far ahead of his age a teacher was is to apply the standards of a later age.

So we will follow through MacDougall's list, with a few hints about each entry.

Fear. This was not the primary appeal of Jesus. And he never appealed to slavish fear, as perhaps Jonathan Edwards did in his sermon on "Sinners in the Hands of an Angry God." Yet Jesus did appeal to fear in the

---

[3] Cf. the author's book: "Jesus—Our Standard," pp. 73-75, N. Y., 1918.

sense of reverential awe, perhaps in the same sense in which Solomon had taught: "The fear of Jehovah is the beginning of wisdom." Thus Jesus says: "Be not afraid of those who kill the body and after that can do nothing further. I will warn you whom to fear: fear him who after killing has power to throw into Gehenna: yes, I say to you, fear him. [Does this refer to God or the devil? Read on.] Are not five sparrows sold for a penny? and yet not one of them is a thing forgotten in God's sight. But the very hairs on your heads are all counted. Away with fear: you are more precious than a multitude of sparrows" (Luke 12: 4–7, Weymouth).

This teaching was given to his friends, not to the many. Likewise to his disciples he said: "Let not your heart be troubled, neither let it be afraid" (John 14: 27).

Yet his teaching constantly made reference to the house built on the sands whose fall was great, to weeping and wailing and gnashing of teeth, to the undying worm and the unquenched fire, to the outer darkness, to the broad way leading to destruction and to the many going in thereat, and to those who at the judgment would call on the rocks and hills to fall on them, and to the wicked who, separated from the righteous, should go away into "the punishment of the ages."

We conclude then that, while the motive of fear is not the biggest thing in the appeal of Jesus (what is?), yet he did use the native fear reaction. Especially are fleeing and hiding, which he associates with the last judgment, expressions of fear. When has the Church made the motive of fear the main appeal?

Disgust. A characteristic expression of the feeling of

disgust, which is the affective phase of the instinct of repulsion, is to remove or reject the offending object. It is probable that Jesus appeals to this feeling in commanding (is it an hyperbole?) that the offending eye be plucked out and that the offending hand be cut off and cast away. Likewise, in warning the disciples against the leaven of the Pharisees, which is hypocrisy. This vice, which masquerades as virtue, seemed to incense Jesus as did nothing else, except attributing his good works, done by the power of God, to Beelzebub, the prince of devils. Rev. 3: 16 is a good illustration of an appeal to this reaction. Can you think of still other illustrations? To what extent do we reject evil because it is disgusting?

Curiosity and Wonder. The figure of Jesus was constantly the center of curiosity, wonder, amazement, astonishment, caused now by his physical presence, as when going up to Jerusalem for the last time; now by some teaching, as by the Sermon on the Mount; and now by some work of healing. But we cannot say Jesus ever worked a miracle in order to amaze people. That would have been like casting himself down from the pinnacle of the temple, which he regarded as a temptation from the evil one. One of the reputed sayings of Jesus, newly discovered, exactly covers the point: "Wonder at what you see!" Zaccheus was curious to see Jesus. Herod was curious to see some miracle at his hands. The emotion of wonder clearly enters into the beholding of the lilies of the field, clothed of God. What we wonder at we tend to approach and examine. So the response of Jesus to the inquiry of the two disciples of John as to his abode, "Come and see," is not only companionable, but strictly scientific. The promise of Jesus to Nathanael: "Ye shall see the heaven opened and the angels of God ascending and descending upon the Son of man," must have awakened a wondering interest. Have you still other illustrations?

Pugnacity. Much debate has raged around the Christian appeal to this instinct during these recent years of war.[4] Relatively few Christians prefer peace at the price of national honor to war. Confucianism and Buddhism have probably made less appeal to the fighting instinct and Mohammedanism more than Christianity. But the fighting instinct may be directed against overcoming social evils by other methods than war. Paul catches the idea exactly when he urges: "Fight the good fight of faith." Jesus probably never appealed directly to the impulse to go to war ("If my kingdom were of this world, then would my servants fight that I should not be delivered to the Jews," John 18:36), though some of his teachings may consistently involve going to war ("Render unto Cæsar the things that are Cæsar's"—one of which was military service—Mark 12:17). Jesus felt that he was manifested to destroy the works of the devil. This warfare he conducted, and commissioned his disciples to conduct. He himself was angered, which is the fighting feeling, when his critics objected to his healing on the Sabbath. So the characteristic thing that Jesus does to the fighting instinct is to sublimate it, to give it "a moral equivalent," to redirect it. So far from allowing murderous killing was he that he forbade even its cause, saying: "Every one who becomes angry with his brother

---

[4] Cf. the author's "Modern Problems as Jesus Saw Them," Chap. I, N. Y., 1918.

shall be answerable to the magistrate" (Matt. 5: 22, Weymouth). What else would you say about the appeal of Jesus to pugnacity?

Self-Assertion and Pride. This instinct is the basis of all self-display. It presupposes spectators, for whose admiration one cares, even while they may be regarded as inferiors. Peacocks, pigeons, stallions, some children, some vain adults, some megalomaniacs, and some hypocritical Pharisees show it. Jesus recognized it in others; he did not exemplify it in himself; there is nothing to indicate that he appealed to it in others. Or, do you dissent from this view? Of course the name of the instinct must not mislead us, we must look at its meaning. Jesus often asserted himself in expressing unpopular views, but upon such self-assertion he did not pride himself. Had you thought we should find direct appeals to all our native reactions in the teachings of Jesus? There are phases of human nature to which he makes no appeal. Can you now anticipate others?

Self-Abasement. If there is no appeal to self-display, there is much appeal to self-abasement, submission, and humility. "When ye shall have done all the things that are commanded you, say, We are unprofitable servants" (Luke 17: 10). The disciples were not permitted to rejoice because the demons were subject to them, but rather because their names were written in heaven. Jesus would have the disciples imitate his example in washing each others' feet. They are not to imitate the rulers of the Gentiles who lord it over their subjects. Because of this appeal to self-abasement, Nietzsche called the Christian virtues slavish. "I can of myself do nothing," Jesus

taught. It was because of his consciousness of the
Father's presence, power, justice, and holiness that he
was always so humble. Are we right in saying that Jesus
appealed to the instinct of self-abasement?

Love. Here perhaps we come upon the main appeal of
Jesus. It was to the hearts of men. Jesus himself had the
parental instinct keenly developed, due possibly in a
measure to his guardianship over the younger children
in the Nazareth home. His was the tender emotion, he
was moved by compassion at any distress, he put his
arms about children, he protected even the guilty. He
could go no further in his appeal than when he included
even one's enemies in the scope of one's love. It was
to him, as to others, the great commandment in the law.
The law had enjoined equality of love between self and
neighbor—"as thyself"; Jesus extended the commandment in his new form to the point of sacrifice of physical
life—"as I have loved you." This is both the novelty
and the core of his teaching. Why, then, does he say
one must "hate his father and his mother"?

Sex. Is there any appeal in the teachings of Jesus to
the sex instinct? He recognized it, did not forbid marriage, taught purity of thought as a preventive of adul-
terous acts, and allowed that for the sake of the kingdom
of heaven some might make themselves eunuchs. But
there is no direct or indirect appeal of Jesus to the sex
nature of man. He appeals rather to its restraint, except
in the general sense that any appeal to the energies of
men meets a more effective response under natural and
wholesome conditions of sex life. In the presence of
Jesus sinful women found the higher love—not the physi-

cal *amor*, but the spiritual *caritas*. Because of the connection, perhaps innate, between the parental and sex instincts, we may say that the prime appeal of Jesus to love would be relatively inefficacious without presupposing sex. So sex is something recognized by Jesus, whose restraint he taught, whose energy his message utilizes, but to which he makes no direct appeal. Is this conclusion correct?

Gregariousness. The company of the disciples with Jesus their leader, sending them forth two by two, the founding of the Church, the free association with men, the rejection of the ascetic life of John the Baptist, all show the recognition of and the appeal to this instinct.

Acquisition (Ownership). One of the fundamental objections to any form of the communistic state, in contrast with the cooperative or the competitive state, is that it runs counter to the instinct of acquisition in man, on which the right of private ownership rests. Did Jesus appeal to this instinct? No, not directly, but he sublimated it, that is, he redirected it to spiritual instead of material ends.[5] He urged that treasures be not laid up on earth, but in heaven. The trouble with the Rich Fool in the parable was that he provided only material things for his soul. The trouble with Dives was that he made no heavenly friends, such as Lazarus, with his mammon of unrighteousness. The trouble with the Rich Young Ruler was that his affection, possibly not realized by himself until his conversation with Jesus, had been set on things on the earth. Lands and houses

[5] Cf. the author's book, "Modern Problems as Jesus Saw Them," Chap. IV, on Wealth.

are to be forsaken for the Kingdom's sake. Merchandise and oxen are not to stand between the invited guest and the marriage supper.

In all this teaching the acquisitive instinct is centered on things above, not on things on the earth. Yet Jesus did not negate the acquisitive instinct for material things, he only subordinated it. Thus he taught that when the interests of the Kingdom had been placed first, all these things of earth—food, drink, clothing—should be added (Matt. 6: 33). Besides, he taught that all forms of sacrifice were returned a hundred times even in this present world. "I tell you truly, no one has left home or brothers or sisters or mother or father or children or lands for my sake and for the sake of the gospel, who does not get a hundred times as much—in this present world homes, brothers, sisters, mothers, children, and lands, together with persecutions, and in the world to come life eternal" (Mark 10: 29, 30, Moffatt. Cf. also Luke 18: 28, 29).

In what sense is this true?

We conclude, then, that Jesus did appeal to the acquisitive instinct for material things, but only in an indirect and subordinate way, while directing it mainly to the attainment of spiritual goods.

Would you modify this conclusion?

Construction. Beavers build, and so do children. Even pulling down the house of blocks is not so much destruction as a phase of constructing again. All men are builders —of roads, bridges, houses, and ships, and even systems of thought. Jesus during his young manhood had been a worker in wood. Upon the rock of Peter's faith he would build his church. His followers have built churches, cathedrals, monasteries, hospitals, asylums. They have organized plans for spiritualizing society according to the Sermon on the Mount. The constructive instinct released by Jesus, as in the case of the others, is directed rather to spiritual than material ends, the material being rather the means.

Have you something to add on this point?

Sympathy. The sharing of feeling is natural. We become affected by the feelings of others and they are affected by ours. This applies to feelings not only of sorrow, but also of joy, fear, anger, curiosity. Sympathy thus is social and it is assimilative. It covers so many emotional states and is induced in us by so many different emotions in others that it is better to regard it as a general or "non-specific innate tendency" rather than an instinct.

Did Jesus appeal to this tendency? Inevitably. Only an isolated hermit could fail to do so. Jesus shared the emotions of others, as at the gate of Nain, the tomb of Lazarus, and in the home of Jairus. He recognized and commended sympathy in the parable of the Good Samaritan. He taught that the companions of the Bridegroom should not fast and be sad in his presence. Can we imagine Jesus at the wedding feast of Cana being emotionally apart from the festive company?

Can you recall other pertinent incidents from the gospels?

To what extent do you suppose the disciples shared the anger of Jesus in the synagogue when the paralytic was healed? or his righteous indignation at the cleansing of the Temple? or his amazement in the Garden?

Suggestion. Sympathy is emotional, suggestion is intellectual, while imitation is volitional. These are the differences between these three general tendencies.

Suggestion is the tendency to believe in and act on any given idea.

Did Jesus use suggestion? Few figures even compare remotely with that of Jesus in suggestiveness. Western mankind has shown suggestibility to his ideas; Eastern mankind is showing the same. Suggestion has played a large rôle in healing, and Jesus as the Great Physician also utilized it. His presence inspired confidence. "Believe ye that I am able to do this?" he would say, as to the two blind men (Matt. 9: 28). He would touch the eyes of the blind, or anoint them with clay made with spittle (John 9: 6, 15), and would put his fingers in the ears of the deaf, or touch with saliva the tongue of a stammerer (Mark 7: 33, 34). These things quickened the belief of the afflicted ones. If such belief were lacking, Jesus was unable to heal (Matt. 13: 58), as in Nazareth.

Can you find other instances of the use of suggestion by Jesus?

Is his divine power of healing to be regarded as any the less because he used suggestion?

To what extent is the use of suggestion in healing still open to the Christian Church? Compare the work of Drs. McComb and Worcester in Boston (the Emmanuel Movement).

Imitation. We sympathize with feelings, we suggest ideas, we imitate acts. Invention marks Jesus rather than imitation. Yet he does imitate and he does especially appeal to the instinct of imitation. He imitated John in having disciples; he imitated the prophets in speaking parables, though he improved upon his models; he followed custom in sitting to teach; and naturally he acquired the Aramaic speech in childhood by imitation, as well as the art of the carpenter. Of course, imitation may be unintentional as well as intentional.

Do you hesitate to think of Jesus as under the influence of imitation? Why?

Jesus makes special appeal to the instinct of imitation in his disciples, sensing himself as their model. "Follow me"; "let him take up his cross"; "it is enough for the disciple that he be as his teacher and the servant as his lord"; "if I then, your lord and master, have washed your feet, ye also ought to wash one another's feet"; "I have given you an example" (John 13: 15). Note especially this instance: "Be ye perfect, even as your Father which is in heaven is perfect" (Matt. 5: 48), coming at the end of a description of the Father's impartiality.

What other illustrations have you in mind?

Play. The rôle of play in modern education and life is so large and so valuable that we should like to find that Jesus appealed to the impulse of play in man. But the evidence is remote and indirect. Jesus must have played as a boy, for (1) no boy that does not play can have the social development that Jesus later exemplified; (2) as a man he attracted children, which no man without play in his nature can do; (3) he later recalled the refusal to play of petulant children (Matt. 11: 17); and (4) he contrasted himself with the ascetic John. This evidence is not conclusive, but it is strongly circumstantial.

Can you add other items? or would you subtract from these?

But when we pass out of the physical into the mental, it is clear that Jesus had play of the imagination, using wonderful imagery, exhibiting a sense of humor, and using wit, raillery, and satire.[6]

Regret it as we may, I can think of no evidence at all that Jesus appealed to the physical play instinct in man. This is very far from meaning that he condemned it. The simple fact is that our games and athletic contests come to us from the Hellenes and the Romans, not the Hebrews. But we hold today that play is necessary to make the body the fit temple of the spirit, which Jesus said it was (John 2: 21).

Rivalry (Emulation). Jesus did not think of himself as the rival of any, but modestly named himself "the Son of Man," the appellation by which the Spirit was accustomed to speak to Ezekiel. To avoid any clash or competition in baptizing with the disciples of John, Jesus withdrew from Judea into Galilee (John 4: 1-3). He checked ambitious rivalry in the group of the disciples, especially between Boanerges and the others, teaching that the greatest is the servant of all. In the Kingdom there are appeals to do one's duty and rewards for doing it, but there is no appeal to outstrip another. Jesus disclaimed the power to assign right and left hand seats: It "is not mine to give, but it is for them for whom it hath been prepared" (Mark 10: 40). Lower seats are to be taken until one is bidden to come up higher. One is to strive to enter in at the strait gate, but not to get in

---

[6] Cf. the author's book: "Jesus—Our Standard," pp. 150-154.

ahead of another. Paul uses the appeal to ambition
three or more times, e. g., "be ambitious to be quiet"
(I Thess. 4: 11, revised version, margin), but not once
does this word appear in the gospels. Emulation is
closely connected with pride and the fighting instinct.
The omission of Jesus to appeal to it is no doubt connected with his omission to appeal to pride and his sub-
limation of the fighting instinct.

Habit. The tendency to repeat an act once done is
characteristic of all living tissue. No teacher could even
by effort fail to utilize it, though Rousseau said the only
habit that should be formed is to have no habit. Jesus
himself acquired habits—for example, attendance at the
synagogue service on the Sabbath, "as his custom was."
And certain of the virtues he extolled presuppose the for-
mation of habit, e. g. putting one's hand to the plough
and not looking back. Can you illustrate further?

Temperament. No two people have exactly the same
temperament, because their bodily organs, such as the
thyroid gland, do not function exactly alike, and their
nervous systems have peculiarities all their own, e. g., the
degree of excitability. Temperament is the effect of these
constitutional conditions on our mental life, especially on
its affective tone. It is to some extent alterable by such
influences as climate, food, and disease. Of course, Jesus
had temperament, and so did each of the disciples, and
so did all the others of the gospel narrative. But all
attempts at classifying temperaments are baffled by the
complexity of the facts, though we still speak of a "phlegmatic" temperament and other kinds. Though we think
of Peter as impetuous, James and John as ambitious "sons

of thunder," Thomas as doubting, Andrew as practical, Judas as earth-bound, Nathanael as meditative, and the others in still more nebulous ways, we hardly know their temperaments well enough to say whether Jesus appealed to them so or not. In a general way we do know that he ultimately satisfied eleven of them, that Peter became rock-like, and John an apostle of love, and that persons of diverse temperaments, except pessimists, have been Christians. In general, we conclude that the evidence is lacking to answer the question whether Jesus utilized the temperaments of men in his appeals.

Or, would you say differently?

Reviewing, is there more in this matter of the appeal of Jesus to the native reactions of man than you had supposed?

Of the possible eighteen, the evidence is lacking for two, to three he did not appeal, three he largely sublimated, and ten he utilized in unmodified form.

Can you single these out now from the list?

What significance have these facts for you?

How close to the bed-rock of human nature do they show Jesus to have been? Yet, how far removed from original human nature in his goal?

Of course, no one would think of claiming that Jesus consciously made all these appeals to the specific and general tendencies of men.[7] The only claim is that his teaching, when analyzed, contains these appeals.

---

[7] See MacDougall, "Social Psychology" for the instincts.

CHAPTER XXIII

IMPRESSION AND EXPRESSION

Professor James[1] writes with italics this principle: "*No reception without reaction, no impression without correlative expression*—this is the great maxim which the teacher ought never to forget."

Did Jesus use the method of impression? How?

Did he also use the method of expression? How?

Prepare two parallel lists of examples of his use of impression and expression.

On which method, impression or expression, do you think he placed the greater emphasis?

Did Jesus rather tell people what to think, or stimulate them to think?

Was it rather his aim to get a system of thought accepted or to develop a certain type of conduct?

Did he care more for the creed or the deed?

People think differently about the answers to these questions and it is your privilege to have your own opinion based on the gospel records.

Looking through our table of contents we may agree that some of the methods of Jesus are those of impression, while others are those of expression, somewhat as follows:

Impression	*Expression*
Points of Contact	Attention and Interest
Appeals to Native Reactions	The Reactions Themselves

[1] "Talks to Teachers," N. Y., 1899, p. 33.

Association	Its Effect
Conversations	Their Influence
Question	Answer
Discourse	The Response
Right Presentation of Material	Apperception
His Use of Scripture	Understanding It
Method of Securing It	Motivation
Concrete, Symbols, } Parables, Contrasts {	Intelligent Appreciation of Truth.

Do you agree with these entries?

Would you add to the lists?

Is impression the means and expression the end? **Or,** is expression the means and impression the end?

Once again, where did Jesus place the primary emphasis, on impression or expression?

There is another way of approaching the study of these two methods. Make a list of some things that Jesus gave his learners *to do*. What actions did he secure from them?

Compare your list with the following:

"Come."

"Follow."

"Go."

"Sell."

"Preach."

"Watch."

"Pray."

"Do likewise."

"Wash."

"Offer the gift."

"Stretch forth thy hand."

"Roll ye away the stone."

"Come down."

"Go and tell."

"Sin no more."

"Feed my sheep."

"Make disciples of all nations."

"Bring the colt."

"Pay the tax."

"Show thyself to the priest."

"Arise, take up thy bed."

"Give ye them to eat."

"Work."

"Compel them to come in."

"Turn the other cheek."

Do you get the impression that Jesus made his pupils inactive or active?

What happens to a learner's ideas when he does something?

There is a sense in which it is true that, first, doing depends on thinking; there is also a sense in which it is true that, second, thinking depends on doing. Can you figure out which of these two propositions is the truer? And the sense in which each is true?

It is true that all our voluntary action depends on thinking. It is also true that all our clear and accurate thinking depends on having had experience in the field in which we think. It is also true that relatively little of our action is based on thinking, though this little is of critical importance. The most of our action is due to instinct, impulse, imitation, suggestion, and habit. Without doubt, when Jesus made people think, they often acted better; also when he made them act, they thought better.

Do you get the impression that he rather approached action by way of thought, or thought by way of action?

If we make action a function of thought, we are idealists; if we make thought a function of action, we are pragmatists. To the idealist, thinking is primary and action secondary; to the pragmatist, action is primary, and thought secondary.

Was Jesus an idealist or a pragmatist?

What are some things that Jesus gave men to think? Make a list of some of these fundamental ideas. Compare your list with the following:

God is Father.

Men are brothers.

The Kingdom of Heaven is spiritual.

The Kingdom of Heaven is social and **at hand.**

Jesus is the Messiah of the Jews.

Jesus is God's Son.

Jesus is man's Son.

The soul lives after death.

Sin is due to ignorance or wilfulness.

Does this list change your view as to whether Jesus placed primary emphasis on the idea or the act? Acts secured are expression, ideas communicated are impression.

There is still another interesting mode of approach to the study of the primary appeal to men of Jesus. Jesus gave men things to do; he also gave them ideas to hold. Did he also give them things to feel? What emotional attitudes did Jesus awaken in men? Make a list of such emotions. What if Christianity should turn out to be not primarily a program of action, nor a set of ideas, but a group of feelings? Is Jesus more of a mystic than an idealist or a pragmatist? A mystic has union with God through feeling rather than act, or idea.

Some feelings awakened in men by Jesus:

Awe.

Reverence.

Thanksgiving.

Dependence.

Trust.

Faith.

Hope.

Love.

Righteous indignation.

Peace.

Sympathy.

Joy.

Would you add to this list? Of course, some of these emotions are complex, and involve attitudes of will as well as ideas.

Is the primary call of Jesus then to men to act? or to think? or to feel? Feeling is an effect of both ideas and acts; it may result from impression or expression; it may also inspire both thinking and acting.

Did people always do what Jesus told them to do? Remember the rich young ruler. When they did do so, why did they? That is, how did Jesus secure action? This is something we should all like to know.

People usually did as Jesus said because:

He did not request, he commanded with authority.

He begot self-confidence and confidence in himself.

His magnetic personality awoke responses.

He was obviously doing big things and knew what he was about.

He had both moral and physical force.

His healings awakened gratitude.

He divided the sheep from the goats, and appealed to the hope of reward and the fear of punishment.

Would you add to these reasons?

In what ways may this study help us in our work?

Would you rather give a man an idea, awaken a feeling in him, or set him a task? Which one of these three carries the most consequences in its train?

Would you be inclined to put "non-Christian" men on Christian jobs? What do you want from men first, a changed idea, feeling, or act? Did Jesus forbid a man to heal in his name who was not a follower?

The following conclusion may not be correct: Jesus cared more for expression than impression. He used impression as a means to expression as an end. He cared more for what men did than for what they thought or how they felt. He himself was more of a pragmatist than idealist or mystic. To him ideas were functions of acts rather than acts being functions of ideas.

Some quotations:

"If any man will do his will, he shall know of the doctrine" (John 7: 17).

"By their fruits ye shall know them" (Matt. 7: 20).

"If ye know these things, blessed are ye if ye do them" (John 13: 17).

"Not every one that saith unto me, Lord, Lord; . . . but he that doeth the will of my Father who is in heaven" (Matt. 7: 21).

"Every one therefore that heareth these words of mine and doeth them, shall be likened unto a wise man" (Matt. 7: 24).

"Inasmuch as ye did it unto one of these my brethren, even these least, ye did it unto me" (Matt. 25: 40).

"He that doeth the truth cometh to the light" (John 3: 21).

CHAPTER XXIV

HIS ATTITUDE TOWARD CHILDREN

A leading modern scientific student of childhood, a paidologist—to use the technical word—has written:[1]

"We have another oracle most closely associated with *'das ewige weibliche'* and to which we can always turn, viz., *das ewige kindliche*. The oracles of the latter will never fail. However distracted we are in the mazes of new knowledges, skills, ideals, conflicts between old and new; unable though we may be to thrid all the mazes of our manifold modern cultures; we do know that there is one supreme source to which we can look for guidance and which alone can tell us what is really best worth knowing and doing, save us from misfits, perversions, the wastage of premature and belated knowledge, and that is the child in our midst that still leads us because it holds all the keys of the future, so that service to it is the best criterion of all values. It epitomizes the developmental stages of the race, human and prehuman, is the goal of all evolution, the highest object of that strange new love of the naïve, spontaneous, and unsophisticated in human nature."

Can you paraphrase this quotation?

Do you agree with it?

Does it remind you of anything Jesus said? or Isaiah?

Jesus was infant, child, boy, young man, and man. What does this signify?

[1] G. S. Hall, "Jesus, the Christ, in the Light of Psychology," Vol. I, p. 275. N. Y., 1917.

Why should God come into human life in the form of an infant?

Why should this infant pass through all the stages of human growth, except senescence?

Compare this conception with that of the Greeks that Juno came full-grown from the brain of Zeus. Remember, however, the different conception of Hermes and the infant Dionysus.

What biblical word, if any, reveals more of God's goodness and love than the word "child"?

Do the birth-stories of Matthew and Luke glorify only the infancy of Jesus or all childhood?

Does the idea of the virgin birth tend to sublimate sex in all parenthood?

So Jesus experienced all the processes and stages of development.

When he became a man, how would you characterize his attitude toward children?

How did this attitude differ from that of the disciples? (See Matt. 19: 13.)

Which of the two attitudes was more characteristic of the times?

What motives led the people to bring their children to Jesus?   (See Luke 18: 15.)

What emancipating words for childhood did Jesus speak?   (Mark 10: 14.)

How was he affected by the interference of the disciples?   (Mark 10: 14.)   (Have you noticed that Mark, though the briefest gospel, has the fullest references to the emotions of Jesus?)

Make a list of all the things that Jesus did for children,

so far as you can. Support each item by an actually
reported instance, or by clear deduction from such. How
long is your list? Compare it with the following:

Some Things Jesus Did for Children:

1. He took them in his arms and blessed them.

2. He provided for their physical wants in feeding the
four and five thousand—"besides women and children."
He commanded that something to eat be given the raised
daughter of Jairus (Mark 5: 43).

3. He healed them. How many were boys? (See John
4: 46–54 and Matt. 17: 14–21.) How many were girls?
(See Mark 7: 24–30 and Matt. 9: 18–34.)

Are there still others?

May he have healed some not recorded? (See Mark
1: 32–34.)

4. He observed the manner of their play and life.

He had noted their game of wedding and funeral (Luke
7: 32), their sleeping in bed with their father (Luke 11: 7),
and the good gifts they had received from their parents
(Matt. 7: 11).

What other things had he observed?

Is it too much to say that here is one beginning of
modern child-study?

With what emotions did Jesus regard children? Write
down all you can, with your reason in each case. Compare your answers with the following list.

How Jesus Felt about Children:

1. He felt indignant that his own disciples should stand
between the children and himself, and so manifested his
interest in their welfare.

2. He used the diminutive of affection combined with an endearing term in raising the daughter of Jairus, saying, Talitha cumi (Mark 5: 41), "Lambkin, arise." From all he did for them we conclude he loved them. Compare the tender words to Peter: "Feed my lambs" (John 21: 15); also Mark 7: 27.

3. He must have regarded them with a kind of sacred awe, "for I say unto you, that in heaven their angels do always behold the face of my Father who is in heaven" (Matt. 18: 11). What does this saying mean?

4. He felt respect for them, for he taught us not to despise them (Matt. 18: 10).

5. He felt sympathy for them. To the women of Jerusalem bewailing his fate, he said, "Weep for yourselves and for your children" (Luke 23: 28).

So some of the emotions with which Jesus regarded children are interest in their welfare, love, awe, respect, and sympathy.

Have you other emotions to report?

Have you additional illustrations of these?

What are some of the ideas that Jesus had about children? Give quotations or references to support your views. Some of these ideas have already been suggested.

Compare your views with the following:

Ideas That Jesus Had about Children:

1. They are a type of true greatness and of membership in the Kingdom. "Whosoever therefore shall humble himself as this little child, the same is the greatest in the kingdom of heaven" (Matt. 18: 4). "Of such is the kingdom of heaven" (Matt. 19: 14).

2. They are not to be offended. "Whosoever shall cause one of these little ones that believe on me to stumble, it were better for him if a great millstone were hanged about his neck, and he were cast into the sea" (Mark 9: 42).

Could this refer to those young in the faith, as well as to children?

3. They are identified by him with himself.

"Whosoever shall receive one of such little children in my name, receiveth me" (Mark 9: 37).

Is this saying commonly realized?

4. They are specific objects of the Father's loving purpose. "It is not the will of your Father who is in heaven that one of these little ones should perish" (Matt. 18: 14).

In what higher esteem could children be held? They typify the heavenly kingdom in humility, trust, and service; they are not to be despised or caused to stumble; receiving them is receiving Christ and receiving Christ is receiving God; their guardian angels do not have to wait for the Father's favor, but always behold his face; while they themselves are individual objects of his providential will.

Did children come to Jesus readily? Were they happy in his company? What does this show as to the element of childhood in his own nature? Did they ever sing his praises? (See Matt. 21: 15.) What was their song?

Plato held that souls preexisted in heaven and at birth came into the body.

Wordsworth sang: "Heaven lies about us in our infancy."

Jesus said in prayer: "I thank Thee, O Father, Lord

of heaven and earth, that thou didst hide these things
from the wise and prudent and didst reveal them unto
babes" (Matt. 11: 25).

Also he quoted the Psalms in defense of the children
singing his praises: "Out of the mouth of babes and
sucklings thou hast perfected praise" (Matt. 21: 16).

Are these views of Plato, Wordsworth, and Jesus har-
monious?

In what sense are they true?

What difference would they make in our practice if we
acted upon them?

Jesus sometimes addressed his adult disciples as. children. Have you some illustration of this? What is the
significance of this fact? See John 13: 33 and 21: 5.

A colleague of mine, a leader in the experimental study
of education, Professor P. R. Radosavljevich, writes me in
a letter concerning Jesus as a teacher as follows:

"I think such a topic deserves thorough study in every
department of education, for there is a peculiar tendency
in modern times to deviate as much as possible from the
greatest sources in our noble profession. Jesus Christ is
no doubt one of the greatest masters of ours, and the
attitude of the Great Teacher toward the children ought
to be taken as a real model for all the Christian and non-
Christian educators. Almost all modern studies in child-
study lead to the pedagogy of Jesus, for here the child is
treated not as an adult, but as a child in the spirit of
Love, Truth, and Freedom. All criteria of modern free
schools depend upon this great triad."

So, in the judgment of this modern investigator, the
attitude of Jesus toward children is the best we know in
education today.

In what respects do we commonly fail to exemplify love, truth, and freedom in our attitude toward children?

What modifications in our practice as parents and teachers would you propose in the light of the attitude of Jesus toward children?

If all childhood is divine—"for of such is the kingdom of heaven"—what kind of adulthood, if any, is no less so?

CHAPTER XXV

HIS QUALITIES AS TEACHER

Most of the books dealing with teachers and teaching, until recently, have had a chapter on "The Qualifications of the Teacher," or words to that effect.

The most recent books have omitted such chapters, and self-analysis blanks, or something of the kind, have taken their place.

In one way it is fruitless to enumerate the personal qualifications for teaching, because they are so many and so general and their enumeration does not produce them. The blanks, however, for self-rating or rating by supervisors, with a view to promotion, bring home one's merits or demerits in a definite way.

We may use the qualities of Jesus as a teacher, his characteristics as the Great Teacher, as a concrete ideal standard by which to measure ourselves.

What other advantages might follow from such a study?

Formulate first in your own mind the characteristics which any world-teacher must possess.

In the following list check off the ones you regard as essential:

The Essential Qualifications of a World-Teacher:

1. A vision that encompasses the world.
2. Knowledge of the heart of man.
3. Mastery of the subject taught.
4. Aptness in teaching.

5. A life that embodies the teaching.

Do you regard each of these as necessary for a world-teacher?

Would you add to this list of minimum essentials?

Now consider whether Jesus had each of these qualifications.

1. Did his vision encompass the world? "Other sheep I have; them also I must bring." "And I, if I be lifted up, will draw all men unto me." "The Kingdom of Heaven is as leaven which a woman took and hid in three measures of meal until the whole is leavened." "Go ye into all the world and preach the gospel to every creature."

What do you conclude?

Have you still other quotations?

2. Did Jesus know what was in the heart of man? "He needed not that any should tell him, for he himself knew what was in man." "Why try ye me?" "And Jesus, perceiving their craftiness," etc. "Why reason ye these things among yourselves?" "Behold an Israelite indeed in whom is no guile." "Thou hast had five husbands and he whom thou now hast is not thy husband." "The woman said, 'Come, see a man that told me all things that ever I did.'"

Have you other quotations?

What do you conclude?

How do you explain the knowledge Jesus had of human nature in general and of particular individuals?

3. Again, was Jesus a master of the subject he taught? What was his subject? Was it science? or comparative literature? or morality and religion?

"Never man spake as this man." "He taught them as one having authority and not as their scribes." "Whence hath this man letters, never having learned?" "And no man was able to answer him a word, neither durst any man from that day forth ask him any more questions."

Jesus revealed the spiritual nature and capacities of the soul in a way we hardly understand, not to say imitate.

4. Was Jesus apt at teaching?

Think of those "unlearned and ignorant men" (Acts 4: 13) whom Jesus chose to be his pupils, and what forceful personalities they became under his tutelage. Recall how "the common people heard him gladly." Note his influence on Nicodemus, one of the rulers of the Jews. Remember that he never wrote, yet his words were not forgotten. Think of the books that have been written about his methods as a teacher. Have you other facts to cite?

From whom have we ourselves learned so much?

5. Did the life of Jesus embody his teaching?

"Of all that Jesus began both to do and to teach." "I am the way, the truth, and the life." "If any man will do his will, he shall know of the doctrine." "He that doeth the truth cometh to the light." "Which one of you convicteth me of sin?" "The prince of this world cometh and hath nothing in me." "This man hath done nothing amiss." "I find no fault in him." "Truly this was the Son of God." "I am meek and lowly of heart."

What is the effect of teaching unsupported by living?

First Jesus did, and then taught. His living is the

tragic dramatization of his teaching. The truth that he lived and taught was, in his own paradox, "He that loseth his life shall find it."

Shall we then conclude that Jesus fully possessed the five requisite qualifications of a world-teacher? The fact that the centuries have shown him to be a world-teacher would be experiential proof of an affirmative answer. That his followers number more today than ever before, and that they are full of faith and works, also shows that in time all the world is to know his teaching.

You will be interested in the following experience. Once, with no thought of Jesus as teacher in mind, I took my turn in the popular pedagogical pastime of stating the desirable qualifications for the teacher. These were grouped under five headings, physical, intellectual, emotional, moral, and general. Then some time afterwards it occurred to me to consider whether Jesus met the previously stated ideal specifications or not. With what result?

I will append the list and let you try it for yourself.

Additional Qualifications of the Teacher:

 I. Physical.
   1. Health.
   2. Good presence.
   3. A speaking eye.
   4. An effective voice.
 II. Intellectual.
   1. Common sense.
   2. Intelligence.
   3. Happy use of language.

        4. Idealism.

  III. Emotional.

        1. Cheerfulness.

        2. Sympathy.

        3. Disinterestedness.

        4. Honor.

        5. Enthusiasm.

        6. Culture.

        7. Courtesy.

  IV. Volitional.

        1. Executive ability.

        2. Willingness to work.

        3. Ambition.

        4. Patience.

        5. Humility.

  V. General.

        1. An avocation.

        2. Sense of the greatness of his work.

        3. Personality.

How would you criticize this list for teachers?

Which of these characteristics does Jesus exemplify?

Did Jesus have ambition? (Cf. John 4: 34, Luke 12: 50.) In what sense?

Is "personality"a comprehensive term including all the others?

How would you show that Jesus possessed the characteristics that you assign him? Do it for each one.

Would you change the grouping of any one of the characteristics?

Why is it desirable that teachers should have an avocation? Did Jesus have one? Did Paul?

This standard was set up for the ideal teacher without Jesus being in mind. When applied to him, how does he meet the test? Shall we say, then, that he is an ideal for teachers, and also real?

Of course, the list given above, made without thought of Jesus, does not do justice to him. What further characteristics,[1] then, would you say he possessed?

A list of characteristics could be made in answer to this question half as long as the personal epithets in the English language, but it would not be necessary. Make your own list of significant additions to the one given above, check in the following list the characteristics you think Jesus possessed as teacher, and compare the two lists.

Eugenic birth.	Love.
Physical strength.	Self-control.
Power to heal the body.	Self-sacrifice.
Skill.	Self-respect.
Tempted.	Sincerity.
Loyalty.	Joyousness.
Courage.	Sorrow.
Prudence.	Intensity.
Dignity.	Anger.
Sinlessness.	Gratitude.
Social efficiency.	Reverence.
Love of nature.	Modesty.
Love of children.	Dependence.
Pleasure in social life.	Prayerfulness.
Friendliness.	Artistic feeling.
Passion for service.	Intuitive knowledge.

---

[1] Cf. the author's book: "Jesus—Our Standard," The Abingdon Press, N. Y., 1918.

Reliance on others.	Alertness.
Justice.	Positiveness.
Authority.	Sincerity.
Love of truth.	Dialectic skill.
Information.	Originality.
Sense of mission.	Spirituality.

Justify each of the characteristics you have assigned him.

What contrasts do you find in his character?

What evidence of symmetry? and of serenity? What do you get out of an analytic study of this kind? Some students reject it as not worth while.

G. Stanley Hall[2] holds that the real Christ is the psychological Christ, that is, the important thing is not the historic figure of Jesus of Nazareth, but the figure of the Christ as we conceive him.

What do you think of this view?

On the basis of this view Hall says artists should present Jesus as large, strong, beautiful, and personally magnetic (Vol. I, pp. 35–38).

Which of these four do you think he was?

Hall also says that the six essential qualities of the personality of the Christ are (1) life from within, (2) moral struggle, (3) complexity and compositeness, (4) exploration of all the higher powers of man, (5) being perennially in his prime, and (6) realization as far as possible of all ideals.

Again, which of these six does Jesus as presented in the gospels possess?

---

[2] "Jesus, the Christ, in the Light of Psychology," Doubleday, Page & Co., N. Y., 1917.

What does Hall omit that does and should characterize the Christ?

Professor G. H. Palmer[3] enumerates the four essential and fundamental characteristics "which every teacher must possess" as follows:

"First, a teacher must have an aptitude for vicariousness; and second, an already accumulated wealth; and third, an ability to invigorate life through knowledge; and fourth, a readiness to be forgotten."

Which of these characteristics did Jesus possess? Was he ready to be forgotten? Why?

Though Professor Palmer was writing on the teacher in general, it is interesting that, in commenting on his second point, he should find Jesus his best illustration, as follows:

"The plan of the Great Teacher, by which he took thirty years for acquisition and three for bestowal, is not unwise, provided that we too can say, 'For their sakes I sanctify myself.'"

This entire essay should be read by all teachers.

Still another mode of approach. On pages 192, 193 is reprinted one of the modern blanks for helping teachers and supervisors analyze personality.

Read this blank through first very carefully.

Then check each quality which you think Jesus possessed, and put a question mark where our data are too inadequate for us to answer.

Make your comment at the end.

Should we hesitate to give in this way a careful esti-

---

[3] "The Teacher," p. 8, Boston, 1908.

To help teachers and supervisors locate their own strong and weak characteristics	Teacher Personality	To help supervisors to help where help is most needed

Name ....

Position ....

Marker ....

Position ....

For checking and rechecking by teachers, supervisors, normal schools before admission and during course, would-be employers, placement and guidance bureaus, teachers' agencies and surveyors

Check (√) after items which describe conditions   Use ? if a further visit is needed before marking

Appearance of room

1. Order. ....notable....fair....poor....disorderly....
2. Decoration. ....attractive....overdone....unattractive....lacking....
3. Windows. ....open—yes....no....clean....unclean....
4. Air. ....fresh....fair....stale....
5. Blackboards. ....much used....little used....unused....tidy....untidy....
6. Number of pupils. ....overcrowded....full....vacant seats....

Teacher's voice

1. Pleasing. ....harsh....shrill....nagging....
2. Clear. ....indistinct....foreign pronunciation....bad grammar....
3. Low. ....medium....too high....

Teacher's physical appearance

1. Vigorous. ....passable....weak....timid....
2. Healthy. ....healthy but tired....anaemic....sick....
3. Well poised. ....medium....nervous....
4. At ease. ....medium....embarrassed....
5. Correct, erect posture. ....stooping, bad habits....slouching....
6. Neat. ....tolerably....bad taste....slovenly....hyper-cosmetic....

School ....

City ....

Personality characteristics of teacher

1. Pleasing .... very .... tolerably .... unpleasing .... displeasing ....
2. Courteous .... very .... moderately .... little .... discourteous ....
3. Cheerful .... very .... moderately .... little .... gloomy, sullen ....
4. Industrious .... very .... tolerably .... lazy ....
5. Sympathetic .... very .... moderately .... unsympathetic. unkind ....
6. Enthusiastic .... very .... moderately .... little .... lacking ....
7. Dignified .... very .... moderately .... little .... undignified ....
8. "Well bred," polite .... notably .... acceptably .... "on the way" .... ill mannered ....
9. Tactful .... very .... tolerably .... blundering ....
10. Stimulating .... very .... moderately .... lacking ....
11. Humorous .... very .... moderately .... little .... lacking ....
12. Encouraging .... very .... moderately .... discouraging .... nagging ....
13. Scholarly .... very .... fair .... too technical .... unscholarly ....
14. Resourceful .... very .... fair .... unresourceful .... unimaginative ....
15. Systematic in thought .... very .... tolerably .... unsystematic ....
16. Strict .... very .... moderately .... lax .... irritable ....
17. Wins cooperation .... easily .... fairly .... antagonizes ....
18. Self-controlled .... very .... moderately .... little .... irritable ....
19. Ambitious professionally .... quite .... not yet .... seems to be lacking ....
20. Teachable .... quite .... with difficulty .... doubtful material ....

Comment of teacher or supervisor—verbal or written but confidential

mate of Jesus as a teacher according to a present-day rating scale?   Why?

Was Jesus "scholarly"?   "strict"?   "teachable"?

What result do you get?

Justify assigning Jesus each quality which you have checked.

Once again, with a colored pencil, check off your own characteristics as a teacher or leader on the last list above, or get a friend to do it.

Compare your own rating with that you gave Jesus.

Recur to the quality of serenity.   MacDougall[4] calls it "that finest flower of moral growth."   The self rules "supreme over conduct, the individual is raised above moral conflict; he attains character in the fullest sense and a completely generalized will."

To what extent in this sense was Jesus serene?

---

[4] "Social Psychology," p. 269.

CHAPTER XXVI

THE SIGNIFICANCE OF JESUS IN EDUCATIONAL HISTORY

At the end of a study like this, dealing with Jesus as the Great Teacher, some of you would like to know how the historians of education, whose business it is to record systematically past educational events of worth-while significance and so to make possible the understanding of the present educational situation in the light of the past, have presented Jesus.

Monroe's "Text-Book in the History of Education," N. Y., 1905, 772 pp., omits all reference to Hebrew and Jewish education and to Jesus.

The same author's "Brief Course in the History of Education," N. Y., 1907, 409 pp., devotes nearly two pages to "Jewish Education," but omits any treatment of Jesus. Each of these volumes, however, treats "Early Christian Education."

Duggan's "Student's Text-Book in the History of Education," N. Y., 1916, 398 pp., devotes one chapter each to "Jewish Education" and "Early Christian Education," but gives no account of Jesus.

Davidson's "History of Education," N. Y., 1900, 292 pp., treats "Judæa" and "The Christian 'Catechetical' School of Alexandria," but omits Jesus.

Compayré's "History of Pedagogy," translated from the French, published in Boston, 1885, 598 pp., devotes three pages to "The Early Christians," and contains the single and questionable statement about Jesus: "The doctrine of Christ was at first a reaction of free will and of personal dignity against the despotism of the state" (p. 61).

Regener's *"Geschichte der Pädagogik,"* Langensalza, 1898, 222 pp., includes the Greeks and Romans, but not the Jews and Christians.

Cubberley's very complete "Syllabus of Lectures on the History of Education," second edition, N. Y., 1904, 361 pp., devotes a chapter each to "Early Hebrew Education" and "Early Christian Education," but does not mention Jesus.

Aspinwall's "Outlines of the History of Education," N. Y., 1912, 195 pp., treats "Hebrew" and "Early Christian" education, but not Jesus.

Taylor's "Syllabus of the History of Education," Boston, 1909, 147 pp., contains the single entry: "Educational bearings of Christ's doctrines" (p. 31).

Graves's "History of Education before the Middle Ages," N. Y., 1909, 304 pp., devotes a chapter each to "Israel and Judæa" and "Early Christianity," but gives no account of Jesus.

The same author's "Student's History of Education," N. Y., 1915, 453 pp., contains accounts of Jewish and Christian education, but nothing of Jesus.

However, in 1919, under the revival of interest in what Jesus really taught, due to the World War, there appeared Dean Graves's book: "What Did Jesus Teach?" (N. Y.), 195 pp. The author says: "The book is simply the product of a History of Education man, describing

a well-known road, when viewed from his own angle."
The book contains an outline of the content of the teaching of Jesus, with one chapter devoted to his methods.
But not even so has the author yet placed Jesus in educational history.

One may properly wonder why the record given above
is as it is. Why do these histories of education, like the
inn at Bethlehem, have "no room" for him? One can
only conjecture the answer. It is not through the failure
to recognize the importance of Christianity in the world,
but the failure to sense the significance of Jesus as a
teacher among the teachers of the world. This failure
may in part be due to the obscuring of the historic figure
of Jesus as teacher by theological interpretations, and
the real difficulty of discovering and presenting the great
Prophet-Teacher of Nazareth. And also those who are
interested in education have not known about Jesus,
and those interested in Jesus have not known about
education.

But the story is different in the case of the four following books:

Painter's "History of Education," N. Y., 1894, 343
pp., built mainly on Schmidt's *"Geschichte der Pädagogik,"* devotes four pages to "The Founder of Christianity."
He says:

"Leaving out of account Christ's divine nature, before
which we bow as a mystery, we may trace, as in the case
of other men, those influences which contributed to his
intellectual and spiritual development" (p. 83).

"Buddha, Confucius, Mohammed—to say nothing of

Greek and Roman sages—are not worthy to be compared with Christ" (p. 84).

The lessons in method he gives us, according to Painter, are sympathy, adaptation to the capacity of his hearers, use of outward circumstance, expectation only of a gradual development, insisting only on practical and fundamental truths.

From Paroz this author quotes: "Jesus Christ, in founding a new religion, has laid the foundations of a new education in the bosom of humanity," and from Karl Schmidt: "By word and deed in and with his whole life Christ is the teacher and educator of mankind."

Among the influences of Christianity on education Painter notes the removal of "the fetters of national limits and prejudices," the attachment of due importance to the individual, sweeping away false distinctions of class and caste, abolishing slavery, overthrowing the oppressions of society, elevating marriage into a divine rite, and regarding children as the gift of God.

Seeley's "History of Education," N. Y., Third Revised Edition, 1914, 376 pp., devotes five pages to "The Great Teacher," considering his life, character, and work as a teacher.

"The spirit of Christianity has led to the founding of hospitals, asylums, and institutions of mercy everywhere; to the establishment of schools and colleges; to the universal spread of education; to the uplifting of the individual; to the furtherance of human brotherhood; and to the fostering of peace among men and nations" (p. 100).

Among the important characteristics of Jesus' method Seeley notes: (1) "It was suited to his hearers"; (2) "full of illustrations"; (3) "simple and yet logical"; (4) "drawn from nature"; (5) "it elevated the truth, and sought to enforce it"; and (6) "it was earnest and full of sympathy." He loved little children. "Every one of the principles above stated is essential to the teacher, and these principles contain the sum and substance of all true pedagogy" (p. 104).

McCormick's "History of Education," Washington, 1915, 401 pp., gives three pages to "The Teaching of Christ." He says:

"The study of His life and work from the educational viewpoint is of great historical and practical value" (p. 66).

"There is noticeable in the method employed by our Lord a twofold adjustment to the needs and conditions of the time. First, the general adaptation of sublime and abstract truths to the capacity of the human intelligence; second, the particular application of these truths to individual instances. . . . Finally, our Lord was the living model of His teaching. . . . Furthermore, our Lord insured the everlasting teaching of His doctrine by making His Church a teaching body under the guidance of the Spirit of Truth" (pp. 68, 69).

Boyer's "History of Education," N. Y., 1919, pp. 461, devotes eleven pages to "Christ." The education of Jesus is traced to the schooling of the synagogue, the yearly festivals, his intimate contact with nature and man, and to the Holy Scriptures. "Jesus became the one incomparable teacher of all ages" (p. 103).

"The immeasurable dignity and worth which these two Christian doctrines [the brotherhood and immortality of man] give to individuality illumine, as if in letters of gold, the function of education as adjustment to life itself—life now and life hereafter."

"The distinguishing obligations of Christian education" are considered under the following topics: Nationality, caste, slavery, women, and children.

"The Methods of Christ" are treated under the three heads: Insight, sympathy, and skill.

Speaking for ourselves now, what place in educational history shall we assign to Jesus? A question of this kind requires an objective answer, based on fact, not personal loyalty or opinion.

The "World Almanac" for 1920 distributes the religious membership of the world as follows:[1]

Jews	14,972,000
Miscellaneous	21,375,000
Shintoists	25,015,000
Buddhists	140,047,000
Animists	161,272,000
Hindus	215,512,000
Mohammedans	227,040,000
Confucianists and Taoists	310,925,000
Christians	576,000,000

The "Christians" include Roman Catholic, Eastern Catholic, and Protestants, 288,000,000, 121,000,000, and 167,000,000 respectively. All together the Christians are over one-third the population of the earth and sur-

---

1. See page 203 for 1970 statistics.

pass their nearest competitor by about eighty per cent. The teachings of Jesus affect today nearly twice as many persons as those of any other teacher. As a simple quantitative fact, Jesus is today the world's greatest teacher.

If we think of quality instead of quantity, and judge teachers and teachings by the fruits of their followers, we note that the two continents leading the world's civilization are Europe and America, and these are, nominally at least, Christian. It was the absence of real Christianity that started the World War of 1914–1918, and the presence of defensive Christianity that saved civilization.

The statement that Jesus, judged by quantitative and qualitative results, is the world's greatest teacher need not be construed as minimizing the work of Confucius, Lao-tsze, Mohammed, and Buddha. These also are world-teachers.

Western history has not missed the point in dividing time by the birth of Christ. With him the new human era began.

The history of education and of man may be written from the standpoint of the protest of the individual against conformity to social customs, as the endeavor of the individual and society to come to terms with each other. This is the standpoint of progress through individual variation. In the main society wins, and the individual loses, mayhap his life, but not until he has raised the ideals of society by so much.

In Jesus we meet in both practice and theory utmost individuality combined with utmost sociality. As against institutions he stood for the man, but for man only as a servant of the higher life of society. This paradox he lived and also formulated: "He that loseth his life shall find it." The loss of life in service is sociality, the finding it again in self-realization by service is individuality. In this solution Jesus shows himself the master of the problem of life. And the steps in our social progress are successive approximations to his solution. This solution he reached by the aid of the Hebrew prophets, Amos, Hosea, Isaiah, and Jeremiah—great individualists all, who found their lives in service of society, conceived by them as the kingdom of Jehovah.

In short, we conclude that the place of Jesus in educational history is central and greatest, on the basis not of personal loyalty, but objective fact, because:

1. His followers today outnumber those of any other teacher.

2. The nations that profess his name, though following him afar off, lead the world's civilization.

3. He lived and taught the solution of man's greatest problem: the adjustment of the claims of the individual to those of society.

4. He taught the highest moral and spiritual truths: God is father, man is brother, the will is free, the soul is immortal, the ideal social order is to come on the earth, women and children are to be honored, the life of sacrificial love is supreme.

5. He taught these truths simply, using effectively the pedagogic arts, so that "the common people heard him gladly." Some of these arts this book has reviewed.

6. He committed his teachings wholly to a choice few whom he trained as his witnesses.

7. He taught from the highest motives—love, sympathy, compassion, and the sense of divine mission.

8. He had the five essential qualifications of a world-teacher—namely, a world-view, knowledge of his subject-matter, knowledge of his pupils, aptness at teaching, and a character worthy of imitation in all respects.   He lived what he taught.

There are multitudes who are ready and willing to say with one of his most learned pupils: "We know that thou art a teacher come from God," and with one of his most intimate followers: "Thou hast the words of eternal life."

To the student: In this chapter you have not been asked to cooperate in the search for the truth as in the preceding chapters.   One reason is that the material covered is outside our text, the New Testament, and the other is that, having come with me so far, you are entitled at the end to know my thoughts not as question-marks, but as affirmations.   This situation, however, need not prevent our having a real discussion on the proper placing of Jesus in educational history.

---

1. Footnote from page 200. Supplemental 1970 figures as given by Britannica Book of the Year, 1970.

Jewish		13,537,000
Shinto		69,662,000
Buddhist		176,920,000
Hindu		436,745,000
Moslem		493,012,000
Confucian		371,587,000
Taoist		54,324,000
Zoroastrian		138,000
Total Christian		924,274,000
Roman Catholic	580,470,000	
Eastern Orthodox	125,684,000	
Protestant	218,120,000	
Others, including primitive		
or none		829,221,000
Total		3,369,420,000

CHAPTER XXVII

SUMMARY: JESUS—THE MASTER TEACHER

What are the advantages of a summary?

What are the difficulties in reading a summary without having first read the pages summarized?

What is a summary?

How would you summarize the essential points in the preceding pages?

The teaching situation is complex, though it may easily be resolved into its essential elements—namely, teacher, pupil, lesson, aim of teacher, method of teaching, and environment.

The conversation of Jesus with the woman of Samaria is an object lesson in teaching in all these respects.

Jesus began by winning attention through interest, then he established some point of contact with his hearer(s) on the physical or spiritual plane.

As a teacher he was not only a tactician with methods, but a strategist with objectives. His greatest objective was to share with men that sense of union with the Father which he enjoyed.

Jesus based his teaching on the vital problems in the lives of his pupils.

Though not a Greek, he was as ready to converse in a profitable way as was Socrates, and he led a more public life, though shorter, than did Socrates, because he traveled more.

He asked and answered questions to stimulate self-expression, desiring conviction rather than persuasion on the part of his followers. His questions are better than those of Socrates, from whom "the Socratic art" is named, because they are not "leading."

He used the discourse at many different times before many different groups on many different themes, but always in a more or less informal way.

He told stories with a point, the parables, which his auditors did not always understand, but which always made them think, and led the spiritually minded to inquire of him their meaning.

He both knew and used the old scriptures, for the nutriment of his own soul and as a common meeting-ground with the religious minds of his day.

He never let the occasion slip, but utilized it as it arose to clarify thought and to guide life.

The principle of apperception is recognized in his words: "He that hath ears to hear, let him hear," and all his parables present the less familiar in terms of the more familiar. Even so, he was often misunderstood.

He used the principle of contrast to vivify the portrayal of truth, concrete examples to bring the abstract near, symbols to make, if possible, difficult meanings plain, and wonderful imagery to enhance the appeal to the imagination and so to the powers of conviction.

He cared more for individuals than for crowds, though he would often minister to crowds, perhaps with a view to reaching individuals.

His disciples he trained as witnesses of his mainly by the processes of personal association, individualizing them, and meeting the needs of each, especially Peter.

The work accomplished by Jesus and also under his tutelage was highly motivated, through the awakening of spiritual and altruistic impulses rather than those of personal advancement, though not to the exclusion of the latter.

In a way most interesting to uncover, Jesus probed the depths of human nature, and secured most of the native reactions of man, though some, like rivalry, he did not consciously appeal to, and some, like sex, he sublimated.

All the methods of impression he used were but as means to expression as an end. Jesus was far more pragmatic than either idealistic or mystic.

Jesus appreciated childhood and made its characteristics identical with those of membership in the Kingdom.

In a way not surprising but confirmatory of our previous impressions, Jesus embodies those qualities of the Teacher commonly set up as ideal.

Though, surprising to relate, many of our best histories of education do not refer to Jesus, by common consent he is regarded as the Great Teacher of the human race. A comparison of his characteristics with those of other world teachers does not alter this conclusion.

As the Appendix indicates, one who was a master of the subject could duplicate the length of this volume on other phases of the teaching ministry of Jesus.

As we have followed these discussions we have doubtless repeatedly gotten the impression that the problems of teaching which we ourselves face are similar to those of Jesus, and that the solutions he found may aid us.

Jesus is the Master Teacher.   Have we made him ours?

APPENDIX

TOPICS FOR FURTHER STUDY

This appendix is a catch-bag. All the left-over problems, really entitled to a chapter apiece, here receive mention only. It is a way of saying what it is that you have not said.

One advantage of this arrangement is that you finally finish a manuscript. Another is that your book is not so long. Still another is that it suggests that the study of the subject is not finished. Besides, it makes a scrappy list to which the reader can readily add, in the interest of completeness.

1. Jesus—a Rabbi.

Show from the records that Jesus was a teacher.

By what titles was he addressed?

How did he entitle himself?

What verbs describe his work?

2. The Preparation of Jesus as Teacher.

The New Testament only suggests this.

You must go to the lives of Jesus, to the four histories of education mentioned in Chap. XXVI, and to the Bible dictionaries.

This topic is of primary importance in understanding Jesus' work as teacher.

3. Teaching by Action.

For example, setting a little child in their midst, the triumphal entry, and washing the disciples' feet.

Some might regard these as object lessons.

4. Accommodation.

"I have yet many things to say unto you; but ye can not bear them now" (John 16: 12).

"If I told you earthly things and ye believe not, how shall ye believe if I tell you heavenly things?" (John 3: 12.)

The reticence of Jesus—the things he did not tell.

This subject is closely related to apperception.

5. The Humor of Jesus.

See the author's book, "Jesus—Our Standard," pp. 150–154.

6. The Paradoxes of Jesus.

"The first shall be last."

Collect them all.

Consider their effectiveness as forms of speech.

Resolve them, that is, state their meaning in non-paradoxical form.

7. The Epigrams of Jesus.

"Sufficient unto the day is the evil thereof" Matt. 6:34).

Collect as many as you can find.

Why may he have used this form of speech?

8. His Use of Proverbs.

"One soweth and another reapeth" (John 4:37). "Physician, heal thyself" (Luke 4:23). See John 16:25, 29.

What is the significance of proverbs?

Why did Jesus quote them?

9. His Use of Folk-Lore, including Weather-Lore.

Is there such use?

What do you think of Matt. 12:43–45?

Did Jesus make use of views for purposes of illustration that personally he did not accept?

See Matt. 16:2, 3; Luke 21:11, 25.

10. The Miracles as a Method of Teaching.

"His miracles are lessons, parables in deed." Do you agree?

Explain and illustrate.

Why did Jesus curse the barren fig-tree?

11. Oral and Aural Methods.

Why did Jesus not write more and appeal to the eye?

Is the ear a more primitive organ of instruction?

How did Jesus anticipate his teaching would survive?

12. Positive and Negative Methods.

Did Jesus affirm or deny more?

Did he develop or repress more?

Collect and compare his affirmative and negative statements.

Compare with Pharisaism and legalism.

13. His Eloquence.

What are the elements of eloquence?

To what extent are these elements to be found in the teachings of Jesus?

"He was a man of supreme eloquence," says one writer.

14. His Economy of Vocabulary.

His art of condensation and omission.

His regard for words.

See Matt. 12: 34; 23: 8; 5: 37; John 6: 68; 15: 3.

15. His Use of Rhythmic Utterance.

Not even the English translation of the Greek version of his Aramaic original can conceal it.

"We piped unto you and ye did not dance" (Luke 7· 32 seq.).

"Every one that exalteth himself shall be abased" (Luke 18: 14).

"Ask, and it shall be given you" (Matt. 7: 7 seq.)

Collect other examples.

See Farrar, "The Life of Lives."

16. Jesus as a Dialectician.

What does this mean?

Collect examples of his dialectic.

What dialectic qualities does he possess?

See "Jesus—Our Standard," pp. 214–228.

17. His Type of Leadership.

How many types are there?

To which does Jesus belong?

See Brent, "Leadership," Chap. VI; Larned, "A Study of Greatness in Men"; Horne, "Leadership of Bible Study Groups," Chap. II.

18. His Living and His Teaching.

Which is primary?

Why was his teaching so effective?   See Acts 1: 1.

19. Aids to Memory.

Is it not remarkable that we have so many of the words of Jesus?   He wrote nothing, neither did any of his disciples till years after his death.   How do you account for this?

20. The Methods of the Disciples.

How did the men taught by Jesus themselves teach in turn?

See the Acts and the General Epistles.

Compare their methods with those of Jesus.

Here is a great field for study.

21. The Methods of Paul.

Study his deeds, words, and writings.

Contrast his methods with those of Jesus.

Do the methods of Paul show that he was trained as a theologian?

22. The Origin of the Teaching Methods of Jesus.

A difficult question, involving at least first-hand information concerning the synagogue schools, one of which was probably at Nazareth; keen surmise as to how the eighteen silent years were spent; familiarity with the Old Testament; and a general acquaintance with the rabbinical college in Jerusalem.

BIBLIOGRAPHY

HOW DID JESUS TEACH?

BROWN, C. R., "Christ as a Teacher" in The Encyclopædia of Sunday Schools and Religious Education, N. Y., 1915.

DUBOIS, P., The Natural Way in Moral Training. Chap. I.

ELLIS, G. H., "The Pedagogy of Jesus" in Ped. Sem., 1902.

FARRAR, F. W., The Life of Lives, N. Y., 1915, Chaps. XX and XXI.

GILBERT, G. H., The Student's Life of Jesus, N. Y., 1898, Chap. III.

GRAVES, F. P., What Did Jesus Teach? N. Y., 1919, Chaps. II and III.

HALL, G. STANLEY, Jesus, the Christ, in the Light of Psychology, N. Y., 1917, Chap. V.

HASTINGS, JAMES (Ed.), Dictionary of Christ and Gospels, 2 vols., N. Y., 1906. Various articles.

HINSDALE, B. A., Jesus as a Teacher, St. Louis, 1895.

HITCHCOCK, A. W., The Psychology of Jesus, Boston, 1908, Chap. IX.

HORNE, H. H., The Leadership of Bible Study Groups N. Y., 1912.
Modern Problems as Jesus Saw them, N. Y., 1918.
Jesus—Our Standard, N. Y., 1918.
Story-Telling, Questioning, and Studying, N. Y., 1916.

MARQUIS, J. A., Learning to Teach from the Master Teacher, Philadelphia, 1913.

MATHEWS, SHAILER, "The Method of Jesus" in Monroe, Cyclopædia of Education, 5 vols., N. Y., 1911. Art. "New Testament."

RAMSAY, W. The Education of Christ, N. Y., 1902.

SANDAY, W., Art. "Jesus Christ" in Hastings, Bible Dictionary.

SMITH, FRANK WEBSTER, Jesus—Teacher, N. Y., 1916.

STALKER, JAMES, Imago Christi, N. Y., 1889, Chap. XIV.

WENDT, H. H., The Teachings of Jesus (translated), Vol. I, pp. 106–150.

WILSON, P. W., The Christ We Forget, N. Y., 1917.

WINCHESTER, B. S., The Message of the Master Teacher, Boston, 1917.